Andrey Platonov

Andrey Platonov

The Forgotten Dream of the Revolution

Tora Lane

LEXINGTON BOOKS
Lanham • Boulder • New York • London

Published by Lexington Books
An imprint of The Rowman & Littlefield Publishing Group, Inc.
4501 Forbes Boulevard, Suite 200, Lanham, Maryland 20706
www.rowman.com

Unit A, Whitacre Mews, 26-34 Stannary Street, London SE11 4AB

British Library Cataloguing in Publication Information Available

Library of Congress Cataloging-in-Publication Data

Names: Lane, Tora, author.
Title: Andrey Platonov : an other revolution / Tora Lane.
Description: Lanham : Lexington Books, 2018. | Includes bibliographical references and index.
Identifiers: LCCN 2018000933 (print) | LCCN 2017059763 | ISBN 9781498547765 (Electronic) |
        ISBN 9781498547758 (cloth : alk. paper)| ISBN 9781498547772 (pbk. : alk. paper)
Subjects: LCSH: Platonov, Andrey Platonovich, 1899-1951--Criticism and interpretation. | Soviet
        Union--History--Revolution, 1917-1921--Literature and the revolution. | Revolutions in litera-
        ture.
Classification: LCC PG3476.P543 (print) | LCC PG3476.P543 Z739 2018 (ebook) | DDC 891.73/42-
        -dc23
LC record available at https://lccn.loc.gov/2018000933

Printed in the United States of America

To the bright memory of Gunhild Garmo

Contents

Acknowledgments

The ideas and chapters of this book developed over a long period of time as the fruit of two separate postdoctoral research projects. The first, which had to do with Andrei Platonov's understanding of the Revolution, was conducted at the Department of Slavic Languages and Literatures at Stockholm University, and I am very grateful to the Ahlström and Terserus Foundation for their funding. I also wish to express my gratitude to the Baltic Sea Foundation for financing the second project *Loss of Grounds as Common Grounds*, a large multidisciplinary project, which was led by Marcia Schuback Sá Cavalcante at Södertörn University. I am endlessly indebted to Marcia for her ingenious scholarly advice, guidance, support and inspiration. It is difficult to imagine that this book would have seen the light of day without her. I also feel so lucky to have had the opportunity to discuss and develop my ideas and readings of Platonov with all the participants of the research project: Irina Sandomirskaja, Leonard Neuger, Gustav Strandberg, and Ludger Hagedorn. Encouragement, comments, questions, and criticism from Peter Alberg Jensen, Per-Arne Bodin, Aleksei Semenenko, and Hans Andersson have also been very helpful. I send special thanks to Charles Rougle for having done a wonderful job copyediting the book. Finally, I thank my husband, Oleg Iliyuyshchenko, for never tiring of discussing with me questions about Platonov, the Revolution and writing, and for always sharing everything.

PERMISSIONS CREDITS

Excerpts from *Happy Moscow*, translated by Robert and Elizabeth Chandler, New York: New York Review of Books. Reprinted with permission.

Excerpts from *Schastlivaia Moskva. Sobranie sochinenii v 8-kh tomakh: vol 4*, (ed.ed. N. V. Kornienko. Moscow: Vremia reprinted with permission.

Excerpts from *Smerti net! Sobranie sochinenii v 8-kh tomakh: vol 5*, ed. N. V. Kornienko. Moscow: Vremia reprinted with permission.

Excerpts from *Sochineniia. Tom 1: 1918–1927* Kniga 2: Stat'i. Moscow: IMLI RAN reprinted with permission.

Excerpts from *Soul and Other Stories*, translated by Robert and Elizabeth Chandler with Katia Grigoruk, Angela Livingstone, Olga Meerson, and Eric Naiman. New York: New York Review of Books. Reprinted with permission.

Excerpts from *Soul* by Andrey Platonov, published by Harvill Press. Reprinted by permission of The Random House Group Limited. ©2003

Excerpts from *The Foundation Pit*, translated by Robert and Elizabeth Chandler with Olga Meerson. New York: NYRB Classics. Reprinted with permission.

Excerpts from *The Return and Other Stories* by Andrey Platonov, published by Harvill Press. Reprinted by permission of The Random House Group Limited. ©1999

Excerpts from *Usomnivshiisia Makar. Sobranie. sochinenii v 8-kh tomakh: vol 1*, ed. N. V. Kornienko. Moscow: Vremia reprinted with permission.

Author's Note

When possible, I quote existing translations of Platonov's texts. Other translations are done by me or by Charles Rougle. I have used the Library of Congress system for transliteration, modifying it for names to make them recognizable to readers not acquainted with Russian.

Introduction

This book was written in 2016, on the eve of the centennial of the October Revolution of 1917. If by the antagonism that it spurred the Revolution shaped the twentieth-century political landscape of Europe and beyond, today it has acquired a specific meaning as an object of both memory politics and the memory of the political.[1] One reason is that because the Revolution saw itself as a break with the past, it exerted a repressive totalitarian politics toward memory. Not only was the official memory narrative of the prerevolutionary past manipulated, the status of individual memory was also constantly subjected to political articulations and repressions. Today, at the same time as the Revolution itself has become a "memory" of a historical event that leads us to ask about what it *was*, the idea of the Revolution, that is, the emancipation of all mankind, perhaps the most significant utopia in the history of democracy, continues to be significant in its afterlife. With the failure of the Russian Revolution and the demise of the Soviet Union, it seems that in the ambivalence of current politics we have been able to bury the Revolution as a political idea and at the same time preserve the idea of emancipation in the now nearly apolitical concept of democracy. The title of this book — *Andrey Platonov: The Forgotten Dream of the Revolution* — refers primarily to the question of memory in revolutionary times, and more specifically to the problem of the experience of intimate memory during a revolutionary period that offered ready-made political models for formulating the experience of the present and the past, and projected its realization onto the future. Yet in writing about the question of intimate memory from the perspective of Andrei Platonov, who although he was critical never repudiated his fidelity to the 1917 Revolution, the book also attempts to bring out an aspect of the Revolution that is often forgotten in current memory politics, namely the aspiration to be a revolution of the experience of inner life in a way yet untold.

This book is entirely dedicated to one of the most complex perspectives on the 1917 Russian Revolution, namely that of the Soviet Russian writer, Andrei Platonov (1899–1951). My primary aim, however, is not to examine his view of the political dynamics of the upheaval. If his writings have often been read in line with current memory politics as a testimony to the problems of revolutionary existence and as resistance to the flawed implementation of the Revolution in Soviet society, I have been guided instead by the urge to commemorate his concept of another — literary revolution as a revolution in existence—that is, in our understanding and experience of being in common. In his deeds and in his writings, Platonov was always faithful to the idea of a proletarian revolution. At the same time as he thoroughly criticized the development of a culture of the proletariat in Soviet society, however, in his works he searched the Revolution for the presence of something other than the historical event that led to Bolshevik power and the political and social changes that it brought about. If the aim of any revolution is to restructure society or communality, what Andrei Platonov sought to bring out in his chronicle of the development of postrevolutionary society was a revolution in our understanding of what existence in a *common* world means. He greeted the Revolution as the possibility of putting a political end to politics—an antagonistic end to antagonism that went beyond its thus far actually realized promises. However utopian this may seem—and indeed, Platonov did not shut his eyes to the atrocities committed in implementing the Communist utopia of the ideally organized society—he was continuously looking for an entry into the utopia of an altered experience of existence.[2] He sought access to the implementation of the Revolution in life as well as in literature, but my focus is on the literary representation of this other utopia of being in common not only as a "daydream" that was forgotten in the actual implementation of the Revolution, but also as a dream of the night, or as a fleeting experience of life that is constantly forgotten in conscious experience and therefore to be retrieved in writing that can reach the very limits of experience.[3]

Andrei Platonov is now known as one of the best and most paradoxi-cal chroniclers of the Russian Revolution and postrevolutionary society, with works such as *Chevengur*, which tells the story of Soviet Russia during the Civil War, *The Foundation Pit*, which treats the construction of the new Soviet society, and *Happy Moscow*, which thematizes the dream of happiness in modern civilization. He was viewed by the Soviet regime as a fellow traveler, a *poputchik* like Isaak Babel and Boris Pilnyak, who were also considered more neutrally as modernist "experimental prose" writers who expressed views sympathetic to the Revolution but who gradually became more and more at odds with the dictates of the Soviet regime and were gradually more and more repressed. Each of these mod-ernist writers is unique in his own way and should not be subsumed under the Soviet label. Yet in comparing them it becomes apparent that one of Platonov's distinguishing features is that in his modernist prose he did not chronicle the Revolution as the memory of a political event but instead sought to bring out the question of memory in the experience of a revolutionary time that inscribes itself in history as entirely new. Formu-lated differently, I am claiming that while Platonov confirms the idea that the Revolution opens a new era, he also seeks a place for memory in this new era as the locus where a revolutionary existential experience of the common can be retrieved.[4] In other words, in the midst of this ecstatic revolutionary and progressive time, Platonov also searches the Revolution for the promise of a way out of the oblivion of existence in common by listening to how things past, present, and future speak to us in different ways, most often through our neglect and sense of alienation from the world. In this respect, Platonov's revolution can be seen as a revolution in the making, not because he was a Trotskyist who believed in permanent upheaval, but because for him, revolution meant the possibility of developing, if not in society, then at least in writing, a specific revolutionary consciousness of our way of being in the world. This consciousness is far from the preconceived model of reality in Lenin's spontaneity-consciousness dialectics because it attempts to grasp how the world in its development reveals that for the most part we are lost to the world, erring, hoping, and deprived of an understanding of it.[5]

Walter Benjamin also stressed the necessity of a specific revolutionary consciousness when in his 1927 essay, "Moscow," he compared Europe and Soviet Russia and posed the poignant question, "Which reality is inwardly convergent with truth? Which truth is inwardly preparing itself to converge with the real?" (Benjamin 1999, 22). What Benjamin is asking about here is not the realization of universal values in society but the Revolution as a readiness to embark upon an inner revolutionary movement and a revolutionary movement of inner life.[6] He twice insists on the word *inwardly* in his inquiries about the convergence between reality and truth. In the first part of the question he asks, "Which reality is inwardly convergent with truth?" and in a chiastic reversal in the second, he reframes the question by asking which truth is inwardly ready to converge with reality.[7] What Benjamin suggests is that the truth of the Revolution must be seen not as a truth realized in history through the Revolution, as the official doctrine of the Bolshevik Party,[8] but as the readiness to ask how we can come closer to an inner convergence between truth and reality. Benjamin's questions, which are also posed as an appendix to political change, can help us formulate how Andrei Platonov describes two different concomitant revolutionary movements. In the midst of the description of the ecstatic acquisition of the ideology behind the official promises of a new society and a new communality, he explores the Revolution as a promise and a forgotten memory of an inner convergence in a common world.

I propose to understand Platonov's quest for the forgotten dream of the Revolution as a search for *another* meaning of the Revolution to be retrieved in literature. This notion of another meaning and another revolution is not intended to suggest an infinite alterity to his conception of the Revolution, but to "de-position" Platonov in relation to the political camps that emerged as a response to the 1917 October Revolution. It is perhaps no wonder that contemporary Platonov scholarship dating from the "rediscovery" of Platonov in the 1960s and 1970s following the renewed publication of his works in the Soviet Union and in the West beginning in 1958, was situated within the politicized framework of the Cold War, the émigré press, and the general political situation at the time. Besides the reappearance of the works, Platonov's reception in the 1970s is marked by some critical reviews, among them perhaps most notably the enthusiastic response of Pier Paolo Pasolini and scholarly articles in Soviet Russia and the West. It is nevertheless in the 1980s that the foundation for the contemporary readings of Platonov was really laid with major studies such as Natalya Poltavtseva's *Filosofskaia proza Andreia Platonova* (1981), Ayleen Teskey's book about Platonov and Fedorov *Platonov and Fyodorov: The Influence of Christian Philosophy on a Soviet Writer* (1982), Mikhail Geller's *Andrei Platonov v poiskakh schastiia* (1982), Lev Shubin's *Poiski smysla otdel'nogo i obshchego sushchestvovaniia* (1987), and dissertations by Thomas Seifrid (*Linguistic Devices in the Prose of Andrei Platonov* [1984]) and Aleksei Tsvetkov (*Iazyk A. P. Platonova* [1983]). In the 1990s, we saw a rapidly growing interest in Russia and beyond marked by the archival works of the group around Natalya Kornienko and the scholarly studies of Seifrid, Günther, Malygina, Mikheev, Viyugin, Bobylev, and Hodel, to name a few of the most productive. This interest has only continued to grow in the 2000s and 2010s with the appearance of publications of revised versions and subsequent new translations of Platonov's texts.

Although the political aspect of Platonov's works has not been the subject of a larger separate study, most scholars have felt obliged to somehow position him in relation to the Revolution. In her 1985 article, Ayleen Teskey compares Platonov criticism in the Soviet Union and the émigré press and shows that if there was a tendency in Soviet scholarship to "rehabilitate" Platonov by pointing to his ideological purity and emphasizing his alleged critique of the West, there was a counter tendency in the émigré press to emphasize the opposite, namely his criticism of Stalinism. Since then, Platonov research has undoubtedly seen a variety of attempts to explain his attitude toward the implementation of Communism, some following the tendencies outlined by Teskey, and others seeking to bridge a simple *pro et contra*. Sergei Bocharov makes a very sensitive effort in his 1985 article "Platonov," where he characterizes the writer's rendering of bureaucratic language of *Sovietspeak* as an understanding from within, declining, perhaps for political reasons, to comment further on Platonov's understanding of the Revolution (1985, 291). In 1986, Joseph Brodsky's influential article, "Catastrophes in the Air," describes Platonov's writings as demonstrating the dead end of the utopian language of Soviet communism, emphasizing as well that Platonov's relation to Soviet power cannot be portrayed as thoroughly critical.[9] And the notion of utopia has generally informed interpretations of his political attitude. Seifrid argues that Platonov's treatment of the socialist utopia can be characterized as "ironic nonreification" (1996, 242) because it shows how the realization of utopia really "fails to take place" (ibid., 243). Hans Günther offers a similar approach when he asserts that Platonov does not abandon his utopian ideal but depicts them as if from within.[10] I will follow this line of interpretation that reads him not against the Revolution in terms of resistance[11]—that is, as an *attitude toward*—but as a complex, doubting and fearing and seeking *sensitivity from within*.[12]

Obviously, Platonov recorded the historical development of postrevolutionary society with enthusiasm and bitter satire at the same time. He repeatedly criticized aspects of the implementation of the Revolution and of Soviet society, yet the Revolution continues to figure throughout the same works as a turning point in history that was to lead to a better Communist society. The proposal of this book is therefore not to write about Platonov's critical attitude toward and/or embrace of the Revolution in terms of *both and*, but to look for the way in which he probed the disastrous aspects of the implementation of a new proletarian community for what they can tell us about its utopian promise to open up the experience of the world as common existence. What is more, the guiding idea of Platonov's *other* revolution cannot be thought of as a different event that could have taken place historically in a different way but instead as a search for an intrinsic meaning of the Revolution *within* the 1917 October Revolution. It is distinct with respect to the implementation of party doctrines, but it does not entirely contradict the official interpretation of the event in Soviet society. The social and political changes of 1917 and the atmosphere of revolutionary fervor both revealed and concealed the meaning of the October Revolution as the quest for an understanding of existence in common, and literature offered a way to look for this forgotten dream of the Revolution in postrevolutionary society.

My reading of Platonov's quest for a forgotten revolutionary consciousness of existence in common is related to certain questions that arise from the philosophy of Martin Heidegger and were later readdressed in the works of Maurice Blanchot, Georges Bataille, and Jean-Luc Nancy. As Fredric Jameson (1994, 78f.) so aptly points out in his reading of Platonov's novel *Chevengur*, Heidegger's concept of the forgetfulness of being (*Seinsvergessenheit*), which denotes the idea that Western metaphysics has suppressed the question of *Being* (*Sein/Seyn*), gives us an important clue to Platonov's understanding of utopia. In *The Inoperative Community* Nancy elaborates on a kindred question, perhaps even more germane to Platonov's literary quests, namely, how to retrieve a forgotten relation to communality, or how to think *Mitsein* (1991b, 14). As I will show in a series of readings of Platonov's works, he conveys to us an image of how the utopian promise of the Revolution to realize an ideal, happy society is paralleled by the utopia of the possibility to remember what existence in common means.[13] After the alleged demise of Western metaphysics, he explored the Russian Revolution not only in its political promises but also in its potential as an existential opening to the world. According to one of his characters in *The Foundation Pit*, "Christ walked alone, and no one knows why, while here we have massive masses on the move for the sake of existence" (Platonov, Chandler et al. 2009, 88). In his attempt to understand this "move for the sake of existence" and why it went so dismally wrong, Platonov begins to ask questions about the experience of the modern world in terms of groundlessness, memory, interiority, and communality in a way that deserves to be brought into a dialogue with modern existential thought on modernity, literature, and communism. Not only does our understanding of his writings profit from such an exchange, but Platonov can contribute to a revolutionized understanding of the experience of being in common in the modern world.

Following Jean-Luc Nancy's notion of "literary communism" (1991b, 72), when I speak here of literary revolution what I have in mind is not a revolution of literature, but a revolution that takes place and can be understood in literature. The question of the meaning of the Revolution that Platonov seeks to answer in writing is very similar to the question of literary communism posed by Nancy, which is a further development of Bataille's idea of "inner experience"; what Nancy sets out to develop is the idea of an experience of the common and communality which differs from the historical forms of realization of communism. Central to Nancy's treatment of the term is the distinction between, on the one hand, "common being," which denotes a collective body that can become the object of a state cult, much like the proletariat in the Soviet Union, and on the other, the experience of existence in common, an intimate sharing of the world that resists all forms of representation. Interestingly enough, if Nancy thinks of common being and existence in common as opposed if not contradictory forms of communality in the modern world, Platonov treats them as notions that are at once similar and utterly different.[14] For Platonov, they represent the two faces of the Revolution. Therefore, whereas Nancy understands literature as the locus where existence in common can be written or communicated and therefore as a disruption and interruption of the myths of society, the question of the Revolution and the revolutionary utopia in literature is for Platonov a more contingent relationship between existence in common and the myths of common being. For him, existence in common is an idea present in the common being of communism, and a literary revolution is in his works a literary matter more in the sense in which Maurice Blanchot defined it in "Literature and the Right to Death." It is a "question addressed to language, behind the person who is writing and the person who is reading, by language which has become literature" (Blanchot 1995, 301). Literature can pose questions about life and reality because, as he goes on, "literature would like to be what in reality is not" (313). What he means is not that literature can be surreal or irreal, but that it can move in a realm of language that is somehow anterior to or in between reality and can therefore also treat or thematize matters, issues, and experiences that are not perfectly real. Literature can touch on life or reality in its aspect of "matter of existence" or "existential matter" ("veshchestvo sushchestvovaniia"), as an in-between idea and material, an in-between the concrete and the transposed in the metaphor (e.g., Bocharov 1985). Also therefore, literature appeared to Platonov as the place to ask for the meaning of the Revolution as a different existential experience of the common anterior to the myth of the realization of common being in Soviet society.

Platonov's literary Revolution can be likened to the writing of a dreamlike utopia, not in the sense of a daydream about an ideally organized society, but as the shimmering matter of a dream at night[15] or the memory of a lost sense of a shared world, the representation of which he constantly looked for in his writing.[16] The utopia of the Revolution in Platonov's works can be understood as the dream of socialism lost to Dvanov in his awakening in *Chevengur*, and literature as the attempt to answer the question, "But where then is socialism?":

> Dvanov began to toss restlessly. He had frightened himself in a dream, thinking that his heart was stopping, and he sat on the floor as he woke up. "But where then is socialism?" Dvanov remembered and peered into the murk of the room, searching for his thing. It seemed to-him that he-had already found it, but then had wasted it in sleep among these strangers. (Platonov and Olcott 1978, 79)

> [Дванов заметался в беспокойстве — он испугался во сне, что у него останавливается сердце, и сел на полу в пробуждении. — А где же социализм-то? — вспомнил Дванов и поглядел в тьму комнаты, ища свою вещь; ему представилось, что он его уже нашел, но утратил во сне среди этих чужих людей.] (Platonov 2009, 103)

In the madness and horror of the postrevolutionary fervor in Russia, Platonov poses this question. Although he shows again and again how the conscious postrevolutionary world spoke about little else than the meaning of socialism and its implementation, he also emphasizes that their explanations do not offer his pondering heroes an answer. Yet, it is nevertheless precisely in the postrevolutionary world that Dvanov looks for "socialism," and he searches for it in his dream because the very idea of socialism appears to him something like the sense of a familiar home in the world of shared existence that only the dream can offer him.[17] Thus, in the midst of the ecstatic acquisition of revolutionary language in the outer world of Soviet society, through literature, Platonov asks about the nature of the Revolution and socialism as the question of how to understand the experience of existence in common in the inner self as a dreamlike experience of familiarity, communality, kinship. The answer to the question, "Where is socialism?" which can also be reframed as "Where is the experience of being in common?" seems lost to the waking world. Nevertheless, like the dream that was found and lost in Dvanov's sleep, this shared intimacy with the world is the other utopia of the Revolution that can barely be retrieved in literature.

Platonov's attempt to recover a different experience of existence in common touches upon questions of subjectivity, consciousness, and awareness in a distant parallel to the contemporary debate on the problem of rethinking the relation between the individual and the common, the singular and the plural in the Marxist legacy.[18] For Platonov illustrates again and again in his works how the experience of being in common not only goes beyond the conscious subject of experience but also appears somehow contradictory to it, because being is ecstatic, tossed between the problems of the realization of communality and feelings of loneliness, boredom, and longing.[19] A unique feature of Platonov's inquiry into literature to ascertain the nature and true face of the Revolution is that despite the despair and all the atrocities to which his writings bear witness, he not only shuns a transcendental subjective narrative position but also avoids the very idea of subjectivity. Angela Livingstone (2002, 402–3) astutely asserts that Platonov undermines the usual position of the reader as "witness and judge" by engendering an "unusual degree of anguish and insecurity" and a compelling estrangement. Platonov is himself first and foremost a reader of the world, and he lets the strange dead ends of ideological language speak to us through the characters' imperfect and ecstatic appropriation of them.[20] His characters constantly assert the Revolution to be a transcendental truth, as if they are speaking from an ecstatic transcendent position in history, but there is little if any space for reflection. He follows the logic of that language to its conclusion, but in the midst of that ecstasy people often start to sense that something is going wrong, and some of them also begin to get a faint sense of their own alienation. From within this state a different perspective opens up, and it is *in* alienation, and more precisely in the Soviet forms of it, that Platonov uncovers the quest for a different meaning to common being. Moreover, he does not establish a position from which to judge the characters and the world, but seems instead to say to us that it is in the truth of alienation that the germ of nonalienation is to be retrieved.

Andrei Bitov once said that Platonov started from the Revolution as point zero ("nachal s nulia"), which is true to the extent that the upheaval was the beginning of the world for him. This is not only a utopian political idea but also reflects Platonov's own experience of the October Revolution—he entered the revolutionary world at the same time as he entered adult life as an eighteen-year-old in 1917. He belonged to the generation and social class that was most exposed to the event, and he received his education and embarked upon adulthood together with the Revolution as a new society, a new world, and a new time. In his works, however, Platonov begins to question the logic of revolutionary time and ask for an understanding of "the mystery of time." He unravels the tragedy of the implementation of the Revolution as a logic of renewal, replacement, and transfiguration, and a qualitatively new point in history that is unable to recover the relation to existence which for him was its implicit promise.

Nevertheless, Platonov asks about the Revolution from within its implementation and its time. Thus, when we inquire about the meaning of the upheaval and its utopia, we must examine the way in which this question arises from within his depiction of Soviet society. Indeed, the inner perspective permeates his relation to the Russian Revolution and Soviet society in several respects. Telling is the fact that even after the affair with the 1931 novella, "For Future Use" ("Vprok"), when he was viciously attacked in the wake of criticism from Stalin himself, he continued both to write critical works and to confirm his endless fidelity to the ruling class of the proletariat. I believe that we can take Platonov more or less at his word when in a letter to Gorky dated July 24, 1931, he defends himself by insisting that he *cannot be* a class enemy because he is unable to conceive of himself outside of the proletariat:

> I just want to tell you—as a man whose opinion I value, as a writer who pronounces the decisive, final judgment on all literary events in our country—I want to say that I am not a class enemy, and regardless of how much I might suffer as a result of mistakes as in the case of "For Future Use," I cannot become a class enemy, and nothing can bring me to such a state because the working class is my native land, and my future is tied to the proletariat. I am saying this not in self-defense, not as a cover-up—this is how things really are. This is true also because to be rejected by your class and still remain inwardly together with it is much more painful than to feel that you are a stranger to everything, hang down your head and step aside.
>
> [Я хочу вам лишь сказать, как человеку, мнение которого мне дорого, как писателью, который дает решающую, конечную оценку всем литературным событиям в нашей стране, — я хочу сказать, что я не классовый враг, и сколько бы я не выстрадал в результате своих ошибок, вроде "Впрока," я классовым врагом стать не могу и довести меня до этого состояния нельзя, потому что рабочий класс это моя родина и мое будущее связано с пролетариатом. Я говорю это не ради самозащиты, не ради маскировки, — дело действительно обстоит так. Это правда еще и потому, что быть отвергнутым своим классом и быть внутренне все же с ним — это гораздо более мучительно, чем сознать себя чуждым всему, опустить голову и отойти в сторону.] (Platonov 2013, 304)

In this letter, we find a key to why, in spite of the fact that because of "Vprok" he had been "rejected by his class" ("otvergnytym svoim klassom"), he still looks upon "the working class" as his "native land" ("rabochii klass eto moia rodina"). Although ascribing such significance to an official letter may seem problematic, the formulation is nevertheless typical of Platonov in that it underscores that he did not want to think of himself outside the common being of Soviet society, that is, the category of the proletariat. Thus despite all the disillusionment about Soviet society that he voices in his works, he problematizes all views by revealing that in them as well there is a longing for the inside. Indeed, perhaps it is precisely because he always depicts the revolutionary world from within and asks about its meaning and really any meaning at all in the midst of it that he also is able to capture its concrete horrendous development in society in a unique way.

As Platonov narrates the story of the Revolution and its implementation, he also chronicles an unprecedented modernization process that can shed light on the course of events in the West. Again, similarly to Benjamin, by inquiring into the experience of the people, what he advocates in the Revolution is a break in the chain of history and the process of modernization and enlightenment. Platonov's insistence on the experience of the people is not the same as the Soviet cult of the people (*narod*). The common being of his people is not "a people" or "the people" in the sense of a more original kinship, but on the contrary a form of nonbelonging in the sharing offered in the modern world. In contrast to the project of educating the people undertaken by the Bolsheviks, the people are also not the object of the Revolution. They are not to be liberated by emancipation, enlightenment, or the appropriation of Marxist historical dialectics. Platonov shows instead how ordinary and poor people attempt to use these slogans in absurd and grotesque ways in an effort to understand existence and to "think for the first time," only to become even more confused and alienated. Yet again, he approaches this people not from the outside but from within their errors and his own kinship with them. In a strange form of de-enlightenment, he asks about the nature of being in the world of the people. The reason is that he insists on an inverted revolutionary consciousness in which their nonknowledge, nonunderstanding, and nonbelonging are the most significant truths about the world. In other words, it is not by telling the people how to think that the world will be revolutionized, but by heeding the truth that resides in their mistakes, estrangement, and longing.

As can be grasped in Platonov's belief in the proletariat as the bearer of a truer modernity, for him the 1917 Revolution means a fundamental beginning in history. In his view, one of its most important promises was to enable modern society to incorporate the people's ways of experiencing. And conversely, he considered the people to be better prepared to enter existence because they were better equipped to face their own darkness. In his novels the people are closer or more sincere in their experience of the simultaneous alienation and appearance of the world because of the way that they *had been* or *were* less in their presence in the world. According to the "International," those who had been "nothing" were to become "all" (in the French original, "Nous ne sommes rien, nous soyons tout"). In his early texts, Platonov sketches out the idea germane to Marxism that in analogy to its ownership of property, bourgeois society had hitherto considered itself to be in possession of the truth, but that the proletariat is now ready to go out into the darkness of the world.[21] Formulated somewhat pointedly, his idea of the Revolution is that we must go from light into life rather than from life into light, because light is the realm of a false image of reality and community. This is the notion that informs his 1921 article, "Over the Dead Abyss" ("Nad mertvoi bezdnoi"), in which he writes that the proletariat's struggle is "the first struggle of consciousness with the stifling universal darkness":

> If bourgeois thought were to sink its teeth into the course of world events, bite into it with the anguish and despair inherent in any passionate desire for knowledge, it would see beneath it an abyss and darkness, not deceptive clarity, not the cloudless sky of truth. It would have to part with the peace and happiness of possessing "the truth" and take up its staff, acknowledge its human impotence and the agonizing, enormous and menacing secret of the world and wander off—to perish or to triumph—to find or conquer the truth. There is such a desire in the proletariat, and its struggle with the bourgeoisie is the first struggle of consciousness with the stifling universal darkness.
>
> [Если бы мысль буржуазии впилась в ход мировых явлений, впилась с мукой и отчаяньем, присущим всякому страстному желанию знания, она бы увидела пропасть и тьму под собой, а не обманную ясность, не чистое небо истины. Ей бы пришлось расстаться с покоем и счастьем обладания "истиной" и взять посох, сознать свое человеческое бессилие и мучительную, огромную и угрожающую тайну мира и уйти в странствие на поиски или завоевание истины, на гибель или победу. Такое желание есть в пролетариате, и его бой с буржуазией есть первый бой сознания с мировой душащей тьмой.] (Platonov 2004, 153f.)

Platonov envisaged the Revolution as a project that turns us from "false clarity" and the "happy possession of 'truth'" to "the darkness beneath it." Truth is in quotation marks because in a bourgeois (i.e., postenlightened, rational) world he understands it as possession. Rational truth, in other words, is not a means of understanding the world as it is; it is an object to be possessed and exploited that affirms to man his potency as the crown of creation. Just as the bourgeoisie exploits the proletariat by its sovereignty, so did it exploit the world by claiming to possess truth. There is, therefore, another "truth," or rather, another world that opens itself to us, and that world is characterized by darkness, impotence and menacing secrecy. Platonov argues that thought must think what it cannot think, or rather, think *that* it cannot think, thereby opening itself to thinking its nonthinking.

In many respects, Platonov's critique of the Soviet world and the implementation of the Revolution is a consequence of his criticism of the bourgeois world as guided by rational and progressive principles linked to personal desire. What modern civilization offers is not a gain but a loss. Platonov insists on looking for truth in the people's ways of relating to reality, which is also his own, and he looks for a means of depicting from within their own experience and sensibility the utterly poor, the nobodies, as the "International" has it, the nameless and dispossessed. The poor appear as a correlate to the proletariat because they not only possess nothing, but according to the Latin etymology of poverty (*pauper*), produce very little (*pau-paros*). The notion of the production or generation of ideas and knowledge as well as goods is central to both capitalism and socialism, and the poor people who generate or produce (*parare*) very little (*paucus*) were nothing in the general course of modern events because for some reason they seemed not to fit into the movement of the age understood as the free and/or necessary production or generation of time or the free construction of the new. Through poor people we can hear and understand alienation, and it is through them that alienation, that which undoes meaning in the world, can tell us its meaning, if only in the whispering voice of the whirling sand in *Dzhan*.

Although many comprehensive and important studies have been dedicated to mapping the peculiarities of Platonov's language and the theme of alienation, confusion, and meaninglessness in general, from the works of Bocharov (1985) and Markstein (1987) to Hodel (2001), Mikheev (2003), and Dhooge (2007), these works have generally been guided by normative ideals of linguistics and tend to assume that his writings are odd in relation to the "normal" experience of everyday life.[22] I will instead pursue the idea that the oddities or incongruities of Platonov's language are rather congruous with the oddity of his vision of the Revolution. I will therefore examine Platonov's language with regard to his revolutionary utopia on its own premises, that is, in how it expresses the paradoxical truth of the estrangement of the world. Thus, I follow Olga Meerson (1997), who suggests a way out of this normative impasse in her monograph, *A Free Thing: The Poetics of Refamiliarization in Andrei Platonov's Work*. Inverting Viktor Shklovsky's term estrangement (ostranenie), she characterizes Platonov's writing as nonestrangement (*neostranenie*) or "refamiliarization," and she shows how in his descriptions he presents what is alien, strange, new or uncommon in such a way that it appears common or is at least in no way emphasized or marked off as strange. I attempt to take this hypothesis further by suggesting that we cannot maintain the distinction between alienation and familiarity in Platonov's works because it is precisely the inner experience of a familiar and common world that at the same time is promised and lost in the outer alienated manifestations of a new familiarity and community after the Revolution. Platonov develops a language to show us that alienation is the common and nonalienation the uncommon state of things, and what is more, that alienation and nonalienation coincide for the most part in our existential relation to ourselves and to life. The way to speak about this relation is odd, and, as Angela Livingstone (2002, 412) puts it, oddness is rendered as an "inconspicuous paradoxicality." In all its sincerity, this becomes immensely comic because it offers a perspective on how we are constantly caught up in all kinds of feeble attempts to combat alienation.

Furthermore, without denying the value of a comparative approach, I focus on the particularities of Platonov's writings with regard to the author's own radical inquiry into the Revolution, communism, and communality. His vision of the Revolution was, of course, influenced by various Marxist, Bolshevik, and other thinkers, notably the Russian Orthodox philosopher Nikolai Fedorov, but to the extent that he posed the problems of the Revolution as existential and literary questions, I will be very careful not to subsume his literary voice under other discourses.[23] It is highly characteristic of Platonov to eschew speaking in an authorial voice with a transcendental perspective, instead leaving the confusions, paradoxes, and dead ends of his heroes unresolved and allowing all their disorientation and alienation to serve as a key to an understanding of existence. He probed the world to find the experience of it in its communality, and we must therefore be careful not to take his writings back to the dead ends of a closed understanding of reality. My intent is to portray Platonov's own unique and singular vision of what it means to be in the (postrevolutionary) world, which is perceived as a reality that both hides and uncovers common, shared meaning. In a series of close readings of selected works I will follow the development of his chronicle of revolutionary society, and from within it the outline of the forgotten utopian dream of a common world. Some chapters or parts of chapters have been published previously as articles, but they have been thoroughly reworked into a whole that can present a picture of Platonov's understanding of the Revolution. The readings are arranged more or less in chronological order, because I follow the thematization of the development of Soviet society in his works. I do not, however, claim to offer an exhaustive history of the evolution of the author and his worldview; indeed, I do not even claim that there is any linear evolution. It seems that throughout his oeuvre, Platonov remained hesitant as how to understand the relationship between common being, that is, the ecstatic forms of sociality that were propounded and abused by the official party line, on the one hand, and on the other, existence in common in terms of the intimate experience of a shared world.

The first chapter, "A Proletarian Existentialist Realism," is dedicated to tracing Platonov's vision of the Revolution in the early story, "Chuldik and Epishka," and the apology for the story in his "Answer to the Editing Board of the *Worker's Army*." Here I show how by insisting that the "coming of proletarian art will be formless" ("prikhod proletar'skogo iskusstva budet bezobrazen"), Platonov came to deviate both from the avant-garde and the edifying project of educating the people that Lenin granted to proletarian culture (Platonov 2011b, 14). The notion of a formless formation attempts to embrace the culture of the poor in their radical otherness to existing concepts of culture. In the second chapter, I present a reading of selected passages of *Chevengur* in which I discuss the theme of the status of the revolutionary and literary subject with regard to the movement of the Revolution. I argue that Platonov's notion of a "better" or more dedicated revolutionary hero is based on the idea that people are able to *subject* themselves to the world of shared meanings. What makes them more revolutionary is that they *are* less as individuals and therefore more sensitive to the common world. The following chapter, "*The Foundation Pit* and the Problem of Time," treats the 1930 novel and its theme of the construction of Soviet society. Here Platonov has abandoned the principle of formlessness for a new allegorical style in which the disastrous consequences of Soviet conceptualizations become all the more apparent. It is precisely in the story of how the building of a house for the future happiness of the proletariat fails and the foundation pit becomes an abyss that Platonov conveys the idea that Soviet society is caught up in its insistence on historical succession and must instead retrieve the revolutionary idea of a time of meaning. Instead of constructing a future home for the proletariat, society must become a home for the negative experience of history that drove the Revolution.

The next two chapters examine Platonov's critique of ideas about achieving happiness in modern civilization. In Chapter 5, I do a close reading of the 1934 novella *Soul* (*Dzhan*), which thematizes happiness in the periphery of the Soviet empire, civilization, and life. The story takes place in the mountains between Uzbekistan and Kirgizistan. Nazar Chagataev, who has just graduated from the Moscow Institute of Economics, is sent to the people in the valley he once left as a young boy to take them from drought and starvation to the welcoming arms of Soviet civilization. The desert walk succeeds in that they reach their destination, but it fails in the sense that it does not lead to happiness. In the next chapter, which is about the unfinished novel *Happy Moscow,* Platonov thematizes the problem of universal love based on ideas of happiness as desire and of progress as electrification in the image of the irresistible and fiery attraction of Moscow. *Moscow,* or rather, *Moskva*, is the name of the protagonist who carries the memory of the Revolution as a fire in her body, igniting passion in everyone around her. However, in her constant and progressive urge onward to ever new adventures, men, and desires, she merely replaces one man and desire with another. Thus, Platonov also shows how a world that seeks to replace darkness with light becomes a world with an "extinguished sky" ("pogasshee nebo"; Platonov 2010a, 19). Chapter 6 discusses the 1935 short story, "The River Potudan" ("Reka Potudan"), which depicts an intimate sphere of revolutionary love and shows how memory after the Revolution is the ground from which their love grows but also comes between the two lovers' experience of each other. The penultimate chapter is about two separate and very different short stories that treat the theme of the second world war: "Inspired People" ("Odukhotvorennye liudi") and "The Return" ("Vozvrashche-nie"). If the first story offers an idea of the power and glory of the war and was published for this reason, the second, which is a critique of the glorification of heroes after the war, was heavily criticized. Nevertheless, in both stories we see how life is felt in the proximity to death and the feeble life of others.

In my readings, I show how Platonov in his quest for existence in common turns from a world of conceptualizations of the own in terms of the same and valuable to view the appearance of the other and the feeble as the own. He does so with the Revolution not as a dictate, but as a *dicendi,* a mode of saying that truly is hampered. He addresses what the classic world (also of Soviet literature) did not want to incorporate—the words of confusion, of myth, meaninglessness, and the people, who are not liberated and not aware and cannot be subsumed under the parameters of modernization. Thus I will also show how Platonov's chronicle of the Revolution profoundly problematizes modernization in general. In work after work, he deconstructs the inability of the ideas of enlightenment to provide a foundation for the modern postrevolutionary world. Platonov's world is a world in which alienation speaks to us, when all that is clear and transfigured is properly strange. He steps down from the position of knowing, valuing and evaluating and formulates the revolutionary question as a question about how our existence in common resides mostly in what we attempt to reject in it and in the way that it resists our conceptualizations.

NOTES

1. The term, "the political," is used here as Carl Schmitt (1996: 27) defines it in *The Concept of the Political.*

2. In *The Inoperative Community* (1991b, 27ff.), Jean-Luc Nancy makes the important distinction between "common being" and "being in common."

3. Cf. Hans Günther, who also noted the importance of memory in the chapters "Utopiia i Pamiat'" and "Mezhdu utopiei i pamiatiu." He asserts that in Platonov's works the future must justify itself before the past, memory, and the constant order of the universe (2011, 11). In the chapter "Mezhdu utopiei i pamiatiu," which is where Günther analyzes the theme in depth, he reads the retrieval of the past against the backdrop of the Fedorovian legacy. However, the aim of this study is to examine how Platonov in his own right treats memory as a locus of utopia.

4. The themes of the past, death, and a forgotten communality in Platonov have often been interpreted as reflecting the influence of the philosopher Nikolai Fedorov. One of the first such arguments is the comprehensive study by Ayeleen Teskey (1982). As Mikhail Geller points out, the notion of the "common task" or the communality of life is linked to the presence of death and the dead, to the ability to awaken and revive (1982; 54, 394). Without really developing the question of memory and oblivion, Sei-

frid asserts that "one of the frequent Fedorovian echoes in Platonov's works" is the notion of "oblivion of origins" *nepomniashii rodstva* (Seifrid 1992, 21). Chiara Mayer-Rieckh's (2011) recent doctoral thesis, *Memory and Wholeness in the Work of Andrei Platonov, Valentin Rasputin and Andrei Tarkovskii,* more explicitly links Fedorov's influence to the longing for and memory of wholeness (*tselostnost'*) in Platonov's works. *Tselostnost'* and communality are indeed kindred concepts, particularly in the philosophical complex surrounding the mythified notion of *sobornost'* in Russian culture. However, I will argue that from the question of the source of Platonov's ideas we must move on to inquire about their transformations in his works. The oblivion of origins means not a mythical longing for a lost past characterized by wholeness and kinship, but an amnesia of our way of being in a common world. The Russian Revolution promised to remind us of this constant and common forgetting.

5. See also Seifrid (1992, 19) for a brief remark on the existential theme in Platonov's works.

6. With respect to political and social change, as he wrote in a letter to Martin Buber dated February 27, 1927, Benjamin (1994) was hesitant as to whether the "Revolution might fail or succeed" in its implementation.

7. Lev Shubin (1987, 129) also notes this quest for a convergence between truth and reality in Platonov's works in his discussion of Platonov's own comment on one of his heroes, where the writer allegedly states that this character "could not stand the rift between reality and truth for long."

8. On the notions of truth and reality according to Socialist Realism, see for instance Petrov (2011).

9. Brodsky (1986, 288) asserts that "what's interesting about Platonov's style is that he appears to have deliberately and completely subordinated himself to the vocabulary of his utopia—with all its cumbersome neologisms, abbreviations, acronyms, bureaucratese, sloganeering, militarized imperatives, and the like. Apart from the writer's instinct, this willingness, not to say, abandon, with which he went for newspeak, indicates, it would seem, his sharing of some beliefs in the promises the new society was so generous with."

10. Cf. Hans Günther (2011, 19f.): "В то время как Достоевский обличает ошибки революционной веры в светлое будущее с точки зрения приобретенного задним числом познания, Платонов изображает в своих произведениях реализацию утопии как бы изнутри, не применяя внешней оценки. [Whereas Dostoevskii unmasks the mistakes of revolutionary belief in a radiant future from the point of view of knowledge acquired after the fact, Platonov in his works portrays the realization of utopia from within, as it were, without applying any external judgment.]

11. Eric Naiman (2014, 801) notes in his recent "Afterword" to a special Platonov issue of *Slavic Review* that "once, the question was how to determine Platonov's attitude toward Soviet communism" and that "Platonov studies continue to evolve around questions of resistance."

12. Natalya Poltavtseva (2005) draws an interesting opposition between the utopia of the people and the utopia of the state, which is not far from my own claims. However, I argue that the two utopias must be seen as somehow mutually contingent.

13. In "Letter on Humanism," Heidegger (1998, 258) defines forgetfulness or oblivion of being as follows: "Homelessness so understood consists in the abandonment of beings by being. Homelessness is the symptom of oblivion of being."

14. Cf. George Bataille's treatment of this notion in *L'expérience intérieure* (1934 and 1954), translated as *Inner Experience* (1988), which is the starting point for Nancy's discussion of the notion of literary communism.

15. Cf. Marcia Schuback Sá Cavalcante ("Kommunismens sömn – noter om Platonovs *Dzjan*. In *Läsningar av Andrej Platonov*. Stockholm: Ersatz, 2017, pp. 81–96) who reads Platonov's utopia in relation to the theme of sleep in *Dzhan (Soul)*.

16. Cf. Jameson (1994, 94f.), who aptly remarks that the problem of utopia must be thought of in relation to the problem of representation: "It is a fairy-tale narrative in which Sasha and other characters set forth to find that mysterious thing they lack, like

the blue flower, which bears the name of 'socialism.' They dream of reaching it, without being able to achieve its figuration, much as in the Utopian discourse itself it is a question of representation in its very content and structure—the problem of achieving that representation that it is to be the narrative becoming the very narrative process to be realized."

17. For an account of the theme of dreams in the works of Platonov, see also Viugin, (2004, 128–83).

18. See for instance Agamben, *The Coming Community* (1993) and Nancy, *Being Singular Plural* (2000).

19. Cf. Nancy (1991b: 6), who interprets community in terms of the ecstasy of Being itself: "*Community, or the being-ecstatic of Being itself?* That would be the question."

20. Cf. Bocharov (1985, 291).

21. Cf. Marx (1975, 352): "[A]ll the physical and intellectual senses have been replaced by the simple estrangement of all these senses—the sense of *having*. So it might give birth to its inner wealth, human nature has been reduced to its absolute poverty."

22. For instance, Mikheev (2003, 4) asserts that "Platonov's language is not the Russian literary language to which we have become accustomed, but a kind of *made-up* language that is altered and even to some degree secret, since it never finishes everything it has to say, in which the author constantly strains to tell us the most important thing but is either unable or cannot decide whether to articulate what it is that moves him so deeply." [Язык Платонова — не тот русский литературный язык, к которому мы привыкли, а некий *сделанный*, измененный и в какой-то мере даже тайный, никогда всего до конца не договаривающий, на котором автор постоянно силится сказать нам что-то главное, но то ли не может, то ли не решается выговорить то, что волнует душу.] Mikheev's argument that Platonov is either unable or cannot decide to tell us what is most important suggests a kind of *kosnoiazychie* or speech defect, a term that otherwise figures not infrequently in descriptions of his language. See for instance Ben Dhooge's excellent account (2007, 85–116) of the debate on Platonov's language as the inability to write in the chapter: "Platonovskii iazyk – nevladenie russkim iazikom," "iazyk epokhi" ili "avtorskii konstrukt?"

23. The aim of this book differs from studies of the place of Platonov's literary work in the Russian literary-philosophical tradition such as N. G. Poltavtseva (1981), Penkina (2005), and V. V. Varava (2014). Varava captures in an astute and convincing way the need to read Platonov on his own premises and in accordance with the "literary centrism" of Russian thought, but he does not develop such a reading in greater depth. My focus is on Platonov's literary observations of the postrevolutionary world and what it tells us about existence.

ONE

A Proletarian Existential Realism

In the dichotomy of new and old in the aesthetical quandaries that beset the foundation of a revolutionary or proletarian culture and subsequently a Soviet culture, Platonov came to develop an odd position. Simplifying somewhat, in the debates on the relation between revolutionary art and the classics that were running high after the Revolution, there was an opposition between the radical avant-garde, which insisted on establishing an entirely new culture[1] on the one hand, and on the other, those who saw a need to edify and educate the new art on the basis of the old.[2] This division cut straight through the Proletkul't (*proletarskaia kul'tura*) movement promoting proletarian culture, within which Aleksandr Bodganov, for instance, argued that the treasures of the old culture must be preserved and transposed into the new, whereas Aleksei Gastev propagated a new concept of art based on the image of proletarian labor. As Seifrid (1992, 32–55) convincingly argues, Platonov's understanding of proletarian culture was close to that of the *proletkul'tovtsy* during the early years of the Voronezh period. Yet it cannot be subsumed under either of these two positions. If we look closer at Platonov's writings, we see that already in his early works he developed the idea that it was not the people who were to be reborn with the aid of aesthetics or culture, but aesthetics and culture that could be reborn if they were based on the experience of the people, which had hitherto been suppressed not only in the sphere of culture, but in fact by the very concept of culture.

Bocharov describes Platonov's writings in the 1920s as "the language of the manifestoes of the time" in which only "the note of his personal voice is heard only as an overtone" (1985, 25). I will outline aspects of this overtone in the midst of a language that does indeed seem to argue in line with the avant-garde for the establishment of an entirely new culture. In "Education of the Communists," Platonov (2004, 62) writes that the past with its bourgeois manner of thinking and living must be cut off from the future and that "yesterday must be forgotten forever." In his concept of the new, Platonov turned to the proletariat not for their forms of production as a model for the new art, but for something which he in the beginning termed "consciousness." His 1920 article, "The Culture of the Proletariat" (2011b, 29), establishes in almost Hegelian terms that the new culture of the proletariat is to be found in "the hegemony/kingdom of consciousness" ("gospodstvo soznaniia"). He adds that perhaps this new culture will have to exclude art (iskusstvo), because art must be considered as an expression of bourgeois culture. The center or focus of bourgeois aesthetics or bourgeois art was sensuality—it was governed by a "passion for/of sex" ("strastiu pola"), whereas proletarian art is the passion for/of thought, or consciousness ("strastiu mysli, soznaniia"). As a consequence, he writes, it may well be that science will replace art as the center of proletarian culture. The distinction between a culture of passion and a culture of consciousness is a significant marker of the puritanism and cult of brotherhood in Platonov's early writings (Borenstein, 2000). However, as I will try to show, the distinction is not, as this passage may seem to indicate, so much between a cult of sensitivity and art opposed to mind and consciousness. Although engineering and craftsmanship undoubtedly take a central place in his works, science in the sense of positivism and cult of rationality do not. His lodestar is instead sincerity or insight. What he really is getting at here is that the new proletarian culture will not accept what he conceives as the mystifications of sensuality in late bourgeois culture, and that its endeavor to be conscious of the world will lead it to bite into these mysteries. In the end, this thought will lead him to abandon the idea of the hegemony of consciousness altogether.

Despite this antiaesthetic tendency in Platonov's early conception of the new culture, his insistence on the hegemony/kingdom of consciousness paved the way for an aesthetic understanding of the world, in the sense of grasping the way that the attempt to form awareness is always hampered by the experience of the senses, and the other way around. Instead of the hegemony of consciousness, he develops the notion of a "spontaneous consciousness" ("stikhiinaia soznatel'nost'") in the short story "Satan of Thought" ("Satana mysli"),[3] which implies a significant challenge to the Leninist spontaneity-consciousness dialectic and its preformulated understanding of the historical process. Against the Leninist and largely Hegelian historical scheme according to which revolutionary history effectuates an enthusiastic, violent movement *from* spontaneity *to* enlightened historical consciousness, Platonov suggests that the Revolution is always the movement of spontaneous consciousness. He will come to regard most forms of consciousness of the world, but in particular the revolutionary one, as spontaneous, that is, as elemental, uncontrolled, and ecstatic. The Russian word for spontaneous is *stikhininyi*, which stems from the word for the natural elements: *stikhiia*. The notion of "spontaneous consciousness" accords well with "The Symphony of Consciousness" (Platonov 2011a, 45) written a couple of years later (1922), where he defines proletarian culture as the readiness to deal with the "assault of the cosmos" ("shturm vselennoi"). The "new humankind" of the proletariat will be an "organism" that stretches its hands deep into the secret depths of the earth. More important than the cosmism of Platonov's views on the new culture is this growing quest for an entry into the world as an organism, a common body of living matter. Here we can discern an important vector in his rather singular understanding of proletarian culture and proletarian art, namely that he will inquire into the experience of the world of people who do not inhabit the world but are inhabited by it in the form of an elemental consciousness.

FORMLESS FORM

Characteristic of Platonov's conceptualization of proletarian art, at least in the early 1920s, is his insistence that when they become a proletariat, the people do not have a model or a form according to which they understand the world, and that therefore the formation of a new proletarian culture must be "bezobrazen," which can be interpreted as ugly, monstrous, or formless. I propose the notion of a formless formation to conceptualize the way that Platonov configures the appearance of proletarian art in his 1920 article, "A Response to the Editorial Board of *The Worker's Army* apropos of the Short Story 'Chul'dik and Epishka'" (Platonov 2011b, 14–15). Published in the journal *The Red Village* (*Krasnaia derevnia*), the work had been criticized by readers for being insufficiently uplifting and beautiful. Platonov writes, "The coming of proletarian art will be ugly/formless" ("prikhod proletar'skogo iskusstva budet bezobrazen").

In this open letter consisting of a series of aphoristic assertions, he criticizes the notion of edifying art on the classical model. This "answer" is both a defense of the story and a kind of poetic manifesto of his vision of proletarian art that is no less important than his theoretical essays on the subject. He begins by discarding the idea that art must be "lofty" and beautiful:

> You write of great chaste Beauty and her immaculate sons who know, see and praise her. You put me among the gang of her detractors and maligners, people who are unworthy to see Her and unable to see Her, and for that reason I am supposed to step away from the home of the beauty of art and not paw over Her white garments. There is no place there for someone dirty like me.
>
> [Вы пишете о великой целомудренной красоте и ее чистых сынах, которые знают, видят и возносят ее. Меня вы ставите в шайку ее

хулителей и поносителей, людей не достойных Ее видеть и не могущих Ее видеть, а потому я должен отойти от дома красоты искусства и не лапать Ее белые одежды. Не место мне, грязному, там.] (Platonov 2011b, 14–15)

Platonov's fundamental objection to beautiful art that is pure, clean, and dressed in white, as he writes, is not that it is aesthetically appealing or sensual, but that its aesthetics excludes life and therefore does not really understand the true beauty of the earth. Those who defend such beauty

> love little and see little. I am a man. I was born on this beautiful living earth. What are you asking me about? "About what kind of beauty." A cadaver can ask about that: for the living there is no ugliness.
>
> [Вы мало любите и мало видите. Я человек. Я родился на прекрасной живой земле. О чем вы меня спрашиваете? О какой красоте? О ней может спросить дохлый: для живого нет безобразия.] (Platonov 2011b, 14–15)

Against this idea of beautiful art, he posits his own vision of the form-less or ugly advent of the new art. Actually, the living and the dead are more important than the categories of beauty that he appropriates for his purposes. This is a "beautiful living earth," he asserts, where only the dead ask for beauty that is different from that of the living, because "for the living there is no ugliness." The word for ugliness in Russian is *bezob-razie*, which can be analyzed literally as meaning formless or without (*bez*) an image or form (*obraz*). The manifesto brings out two possible meanings that are more apparent in the adjectival or adverbial forms that he will use to describe the coming of proletarian culture: *bezobraznyi* or *bezobrazen*. *Bezobraznyi* shifts in meaning, depending on the stress; *bezo-braznyi* means ugly, monstrous, or unsuitable, whereas *bezobraznyi* means without an image, formless. The coming of proletarian art is conceived as ugly or monstrous because it has no image, model, or form.[4] Moreover, Platonov senses in the word *bezobraznyi* (formless) the notion of a lack of education (*obrazovanie*), which like the German word *Bildung* is built on the stem meaning image—*obraz* (*Bild*). The people do not have the privi-leged classes' established forms of education and formation to be able to appreciate art, and therefore they and their art will appear monstrous or ugly. But it is in the lack of a model or form that their art and aesthetics of living beauty will reside. In becoming a culture, the proletariat (or peo-ple) must neither appropriate the already established models, forms, or images nor create the new, but somehow be faithful to their own defor-mity and formlessness. The aim of describing the coming of proletarian art as formless is that this art must remain faithful to the people in their errancy. In other words, even a couple of years before he enters the Pro-letkul't movement, we can see in this article that Platonov is not inter-ested in ideological constructions and that his attention is entirely dedicated to the search for the actual forms of the coming culture of the poor or of the coming of their poor culture. Moreover, the advent of proletarian art does not appear solely as the emergence of a different hegemonic political class, which was a central idea for Bogdanov and the Proletkul't. What is approaching instead is the way in which life itself will speak from the perspective of its alienated rejection from culture, and this must to some extent be a formless form. Thus, Platonov circumvents the impossible opposition between the ideals of the Soviet project to "educate the people" and the images with which the people themselves understood the world. Only when proletarian art becomes culture without an image can it herald the arrival of the new times.

"CHUL'DIK AND EPISHKA"

Before continuing with my close reading of Platonov's "manifesto," I will sketch out the two-page story that motivated it. The plot tells the rather gloomy and sad tale of the fisherman Epishka and his daughter, who are killed in a fire in a rather simple and straightforward manner. Here as well, however, we find some overtones of Platonov's voice. Beginning on the banks of the River Don and climaxing in the village, the narrative is dominated by the two elements: fire and water. Water and the river flow harmoniously, whereas fire is a hostile and destructive force. The story begins with Epishka, who is described as malicious or snarky (ekhidnyi),[5] dreaming that he is having a great meal and embracing someone else's woman in the hay. As a result of his critique of the hegemony of the "passion for/of sex" ("strastiu pola"), desire is not infrequently portrayed as evil, particularly in his early works. As Philip Ross Bullock remarks in *The Feminine in the Prose of Andrei Platonov*, in the 1920s Platonov conceived of a fundamental opposition between the revolutionary cause and sexual desire (2005, 4) .[6] Here this opposition takes the form of a conflict in Epishka, who because of his desire, becomes forgetful of the world and his kin. When Chul'dik wakes him up to warn him that something seems to be wrong in his hut, he starts to groan and yell at the imagined woman. His dream and sleep show him to be distraught and subject to desires that confuse him. When he comes to his senses and sees that there is a fire, he hurries home, but in all his movements there is a sense of being lost, which is rendered through the elements of fire and air:

> Epishka, whose malicious eye was sharp, burned deep inside with grief, and off he went across the Don as fast as he could. On the other side Epishka grabbed a bush and hung on it, weakened.

> [У Епишки, который был зорок на ехидный глаз, горело от горя сердце, и он дул через Дон во всю мочь. На том боку Епишка ухватился за куст и повис на нем, ослабши.] (Platonov 2011b, 30).[7]

The fire blazes as hotly deep within Epishka as it does outside him. That his "heart burned with grief" ("gorelo ot goria serdtse") might seem to be a rather conventional metaphor, but it allows for the crucial transfers of meaning that are so typical of Platonov's existential landscape, where experience of the world and the world itself coincide. At first the fire is present in a rather traditional form of metaphorical speech, with a transfer of epithets from nature to man. Subsequently, however, there is an inverse transfer from images of the soul or feelings to external reality. Epishka's dry and burning heart will cause the landscape to dry out and burn. Thus, in a manner that is distantly reminiscent of natural spiritism, Platonov underscores already in his early works that man cannot be separated from the nature that he inhabits. As we will see, Epishka runs and hurries "as fast as he can" (or with all this might—vo vsiu moch') . We are told that he hangs on the branch by the shore "weakened/worn out" ("oslabshi"), but we also learn that he is losing or has lost his spirit and soul:

> There he goes, rushing spiritless around the meadow holding up his pants by the fly. Yonder is his hut. His little girl is sleeping there in her cradle. She is wet and wants to eat. But he, Epishka, roams over the hot dry fields and thinks about who knows what, living without friends, without kin and with no haven.

> [Вот он без духа летит по лугу и держит штаны за ширинку. Вонна его хата. Там спит его девочка в люльке. Она обмокла и хочет есть. А он, Епишка, бродит один по жарким сухим полям и думает неведомо о чем, живет без друга, без родного человека и без причалу.] (30)

The overtones of Platonov's style can be heard in the unassuming fusion of language registers, perspectives, and meanings. Epishka runs home not breathless, but "spiritless" to where his daughter is wet and hungry. The reason for this lack of spirit is further evident in the way that he has been wandering aimlessly and alone over the hot dry fields. Thus, without explaining why or providing any chain of cause and effect but simply through juxtaposition, Platonov is saying that nature testifies to the condition of man as much as the other way around. The elements are constantly present as a connection between man and nature. The world is an organism in Platonov's works; man is the movement of nature as much as the movements of nature are man. The fields are hot and dry, while Epishka wanders about without friends, a home, or a safe haven. In other words, the implied drought is equated with his homelessness in the world through neither metaphorization nor any consequential chain, but by suggesting that the dryness has intensified because he has been wandering about thinking only of himself and neglecting the world. Having established a connection between the dry fields and Epishka's inner drought, Platonov goes on to assert that he has a "dry heart" ("sukhoe serdtse"):

> Now the fire has spread to his hut from the neighboring wattle fence, and Epishka rushes around and feels his soul collapse, the blood stands still in his veins, and his dry heart dance. The whole neighborhood is deserted. Half the village is in flames. And Epishka, white as a stone fallen from an alien sky, lay there dead and accursed.
>
> [Теперь его хата занялась полымем от соседского плетня, и Епишка вот мчится и чует, как проваливается его душа, как стоит кровь в жилах и пляшет сухое сердце. По всей округе было безлюдье. Полсела полыхало. А Епишка, белый как камень с чужого неба, лежал мертвым и окаянным.] (30)

Although Epishka dashes around (mchitsia), he senses that his soul is foundering, and his dry heart is dancing. He has no force to oppose the fire that is spreading because the drought is devouring him. In the end, therefore, he falls down, "dead and accursed" (okaiannyi). The word *okaiannyi*, which has strong religious connotations, underscores his own responsibility for events. Although the story does not give us any reason to read this condemnation in any strictly religious key, it does point to a kind of existential cursedness. In other words, in his way of being in the world he is lost to the world.[8] Because he does not sense the aridity of his loneliness, he is powerless against fire, which feeds on drought. Epishka's greed and dryness are contrasted to Chul'dik, who is at one with the element of water:

> The Don flowed over its shoals, and Chul'dik sat in the boat in the middle of the river threading worms on his hooks. He was at home there, taking nourishment from the river and thinking about it.
>
> [Дон лился на перекатах, и Чульдик сидел в лодке середь реки и нанизывал червей на крючки. Он был там свой, питаясь из реки и думая над ней.] (30)

While Epishka is running home, Chul'dik is sitting in his boat "in the middle of the river" ("sered' reki"). As opposed to Epishka, Chul'dik is not alienated from the landscape; he is *in* this element, as if embraced by it. There, he is at home ("On byl tam svoi"), and he is nurtured by the river and thinks only of it. A couple of days later, Chul'dik buries Epishka and, satisfied with his work, concludes that the issue has been put to an end ("delo s kontsom"). After a while, Epishka appears to him in a dream. When Chul'dik later visits him at the graveyard, he now calls him *Kuzma*, which stems from the Greek word for world (*kosmos*), and he turns to him, "pitiless," and asks him, why he "hurt its idol" ("idol ee rashshib"). This time, in an echo and rhythmic parallel to the image of Chul'dik in the boat, the world answers him as follows:

The Don muttered over its shoals, and the black hole of the hut could
be seen on the other bank. On the street of the village an accordion
bawled and sneered to the singing of the women:
>It doesn't matter what I am,
>Stay away from me, you creep!
>I'm my own woman,
>And a man's nothing new to me.

[Дон бормотал на перекатах и видна была черная дыра землянки
на том берегу. На улице рвала и ухмылялась гармошка под лад
девок:
>Я какая ни на есть —
>Ко мне, гадина, не лезь!
>Я сама себе головка,
>А мужик мне не обновка!] (31)

If in the parallel image at the end of the previous passage the Don was
"running" or "flowing" ("lilsia") over its shoals, now it is "muttering"
("bormotal"), and the "black hole" where Chul'dik was sleeping is vis-
ible. The vision is now much more hostile. The world is tuned in a completely different way, and the reason is that another, uncanny voice is
heard: the voice of the shattered world. Life as a "free thing"[9] appears in
its opposition to the forms of human possession, and it does so in a rather
inhospitable world.

THE SIGNIFICANCE OF THE MOSQUITO: THE MANIFESTO

In this rather simple story, we can still discern Platonov's specific focus
on the world. He understands us humans in the way that we exist ecstatically in the world and are possessed by our surroundings, which appear
to and affect us as elements. This insistence on our way of being is also
what motivates his resistance to art that is edifying and beautiful. Because the new art must grasp human beings from within their utter vul-
nerability and helplessness, it will be characterized by ugliness and formlessness. However, he finds a richness in the experience of living in cultural poverty. As he writes in his "manifesto,"

>I know that I am one of the most insignificant. That you have correctly
>noticed. But I also know that the more insignificant the creature, the
>more delighted it is with life, because it is least of all worthy of it. The
>tiniest mosquito is the happiest soul. The more insignificant the crea-
>ture, the more beautiful and greater is its soul. This you were unable to
>note. You are legitimate and worthy people, while I just want to be-
>come human. For you being human is a habit, but for me it is a rarity
>and a holiday.

>[Я знаю, что я один из самых ничтожных. Это вы верно заметили.
>Но я знаю еще, чем ничтожней существо, тем оно больше радо

жизни, потому что менее всего достойно ее. Самый маленький комарик самая счастливая душа. Чем ничтожней существо, тем прекраснее и больше душа его. Этого вы не могли подметить. Вы люди законные и достойные, я человеком только хочу быть. Для вас быть человеком привычка, для меня редкость и праздник.] ((Platonov 2011b, 15)

The tone of this utterly sincere apology of his art is of course sarcastic and mocking. He takes the position of an outsider not only to society, but in fact also to the universal concept of humanity. The reason is that in his critique of culture, the outside is really the inside of life. He is an outsider to the alienated claim to possess the inside, because more can be felt outside than inside. He aligns himself with a mosquito because the mosquito is really the happiest creature and has the most beautiful and greatest soul. He himself is not really human: he only "wants to be human," and it is a rare feast for him to be so. Humanity belongs to the parameters of value: it is associated with dignity and law, but for Platonov, life and soulfulness reside in what is insignificant and outside of humanity, dignity, and value. His "outsidedness" is not rooted in a marginalized and elitist opposition to popular culture. Although it is formed in the margins of society, it is outside of a society that is unable to include the proletariat, which is defined as lacking material means and thus also any access to the future as such. Society will constantly seek to educate and reform the people within the parameters of civilization and culture, but what Platonov cherishes is being true to the experience of insignificant outsidedness. When he goes on to elaborate on this outside position, he does so in the name of proletarian art. His outside position is the position of nontruth, nonbeauty, and nonform that has no value but in the way that it is everything, in the way that it *is*:

> I am convinced that the coming of proletarian art will be ugly/formless. We grow out of the earth, out of all its filth, and everything that is on the earth is on us as well. But never fear; we will cleanse ourselves, we hate our squalor, we insist on moving out of the dirt. Therein lies our meaning. Out of our ugliness the soul of the world is growing.
>
> [Я уверен, что приход пролетарского искусства будет безобразен. Мы растем из земли, из всех ее нечистот, и все, что есть на земле, есть и на нас. Но не бойтесь, мы очистимся, мы ненавидим свое убожество, мы упорно идем из грязи. В этом наш смысл. Из нашего уродства вырастает душа мира.] (Platonov 2011b, 15)

Platonov's understanding of proletarian art is that at least at its arrival (prikhod), it must be ugly or formless (*bezobrazen*). As mentioned above, the short form of the adjective *bezobrazen*, means not only mean, ugly, abominable and even undignified, but also without (*bez*) form or image (*obraz*). This double meaning expresses well Platonov's idea of the life of the proletariat, which precisely in its lack of forms of representation is the *all* of the earth. In his description of this undignified formlessness, he identifies himself and the proletariat with all that is most abject.[10] He is dirty (*griaznyi*) and insignificant (*nichtozhnyi*); he represents squalor (*ubozhestvo*), deformity (*urodstvo*), and first and foremost, the formless or abominable (*bezobrazie*). However, it is precisely by being the weeds of the earth that proletarian art will be all—the "soul of the earth" ("dusha mira"), the title of an article written the same year. The abject is the locus of the all, and Platonov writes, "We grow out of the earth, from all its filth, and all that is on earth, is on us as well" ("My rastem iz zemli, iz vsekh ee nechistot, i vse, chto est' na zemle, est' i na nas") (2011b, 15).

Interesting in this passage is the notion of change, the idea of a *coming*. In his opposition to culture and human dignity, what can such an advent be? Platonov writes, "But never fear; we will cleanse ourselves, we hate our squalor, we insist on moving out of the dirt" (Platonov 2011b, 15). "This is the proletarians' "meaning," that is, the meaning of their existence, and this is how "the soul of the earth" will grow out of them. Now, on this point, Platonov is contradictory and will remain uncertain.[11] Is there a possible transition from the formless to form in which the soul of the most dispossessed, formless and insignificant is preserved? This is a question that will resound throughout his oeuvre. According to the society of the dignified, of humanity, people must go from filth to beauty, but Platonov insists that there is "no ugliness" ("net bezobraziia") for the living. Therefore, in their transition from formlessness/ugliness to form, the sense of the formless living must be preserved, as must the understanding of how their errancy testifies to a search. He continues:

> You see only our errors and cannot understand that we are not erring but searching. We are coming from below. Help us, you above. That is my answer. There is no ugliness for the living.
>
> [Вы видите только наши заблуждения, а не можете понять, что не блуждаем мы, а ищем. Мы идем снизу, помогите нам, верхние, в этом мой ответ. Для живого нет безобразия.] (Platonov 2011b, 15)

The truth of the people is their untruth; their road is the path of error, and where they may end remains unspoken.

Crucial here is not the indeterminateness of the people's destination, but the idea that their "truth is their untruth." The maxim that "the coming of proletarian art will be ugly/formless" ought to be interpreted not so much as an avant-garde or modernist experiment in formless form, but as the need to understand and shape a narrative that can incorporate the people in their errors and untruths *as truths*. There is no other truth but the truth of the untruth of the people, in other words—only their errors and sense of insignificant outsidedness can speak to us about the world in its own right and on its own terms. Thus, the possibility of a proletarian art for Platonov is the possibility of acknowledging errors and the formless in their own right. Therefore, he will also develop a form of narrative in which he is able to let the errors of the realization of the Revolution reveal the truth about it.

A REALISM OF FORMLESS INSIGNIFICANCE

Formlessness is a property of the proletarian consciousness and way of living, and proletarian art is defined by doing justice to that formlessness. This principle undoubtedly has a bearing on the narrative mode of Platonov's stories. As is reflected in a prose without any clear story or narrative line, his characters often heedlessly and aimlessly follow the whims of fate. However, one can argue that the basis for his writing is a realism of sorts. Indeed, in the maxim "for the living there is nothing ugly/formless/ undignified" we can see the beginning of a proletarian existentialist realism that differs from Socialist Realism. If the latter in many respects can be defined as an idealistic realism, Platonov's proletarian realism cherishes the insignificant reality of what is forgotten and rejected in people:

> Not to seem great, but to be oneself is a very important thing that no one values. To live, not to dream, to see, not to imagine. Art is beyond people's capacity, but on the other hand it is the only true art.
>
> [Не казаться большим, а быть каким есть — очень важная никем не ценимая вещь. Жить, а не мечтать, видеть, а не воображать — искусство не по силе людей, но зато и единственно истинное искусство.] (Platonov 2011b, 15)

Platonov writes that art must "live" and not "dream," "see" rather than "imagine." The stem of the word *bezobraznyi* (formless, ugly) is *obraz* (image), which is also present in *voobrazhat'* ("to imagine"). He may seem more traditionally realist than he actually is in this passage, but the point is not to mirror reality or to be objective in any conventional realist sense. What he is insisting on is the nearly utopian difficulty of writing about reality in its ugly worthlessness. A related idea is expressed in the 1921 article, "The Soul of Man is an Indecent Animal" ("Dusha cheloveka — neprilichnoe zhivotnoe"), where Platonov similarly contrasts himself to the status of ideals of beauty in Soviet culture (and elsewhere):

> He knew only one thing: these trifles are the whole truth of life. The ideal, spirit and the skirts of old maids are merely matter gone astray.
>
> [Он знал одно: эти мелочи — вся истина жизни. Идеал, дух и прочие юбки старых дев это суть только заблуждающаяся материя.] (Platonov 2011b, 607)

It may perhaps seem inadequate to compare something Platonov wrote in the Voronezh period to the doctrine for Soviet art that was officially established only in 1934. Yet what he reacts to and rejects in this manifesto is precisely the desire to find edifying art in the doctrine. If Socialist Realism is a pedagogical guidebook for ideological awareness in which all details are significant and lead to the correct insight, [12] what Platonov attempts to do at the advent of proletarian culture is to write the meaning of the meaningless and insignificant that exists beyond any "humanist" or "realist" value.

As a consequence of this vision of proletarian art, which was to focus on the insignificant as a locus for the real and for meaning, Platonov developed a specific form of writing that is absurdist, grotesque, and phantasmagorical. Yet he himself insists on the meaningless, the ugly, and the trivial as reality, and there is a case for arguing that his attention to the insignificant is a form of realism—a realism that goes beyond the tendency toward the universalist idealism of realist instruction. In any event, there is a precedent in realism for attempting to underscore the common sense of reality by opposing it to the real of the insignificant. As the American structuralist Jonathan Culler (2007) astutely frames it in "The Realism of *Madame Bovary*," there is a realism "as the *effet de réel*, the confrontation with the facticity of a world that is just there, resistant to signification." He is referring to Barthes's (1968, 84–89) famous essay, "L'Effet de reél," which describes the "representation of the real" in terms of the way in which the concrete detail, precisely because of its resistance to meaning, "becomes the sufficient justification for speaking" in realism. Barthes stresses that it is as if realism assumes "that what is alive cannot signify." Although this trait in Flaubert would be connected in Soviet scholarship and elsewhere primarily with Formalism's preoccupation with concrete details, a focus on the insignificance of the living finds a very specific treatment in the realism of Platonov's works.

Platonov insists on the insignificant in life: concrete details, people, or mishaps as the truth about the reality of meaning and how our understanding of meaning often leads us astray. What has meaning in his world is what is alive and has very little or no meaning in reality and very little significance in the narrative. In other words, Platonov writes his proletarian realist prose when he turns to things that are ascribed no value and no significance by attempting to come closer to the *meaning* of the insignificant in the modern world. He searches for a means of portraying people whose alienation bespeaks a forgotten value. Very radically and yet timidly, Platonov tells us that there is no truth, no form, no art, and ultimately, no life to possess and to make your own. [13] The artistic impulse here that was crucial for Platonov was to write a living, seeing, or hearing of the formless and really nonseeing errancy of the people—to show them in the meaning and truth of their incapacity to think or, like Kopenkin in *Chevengur*, "to use their heads," or their inability to lay a foundation on which to build anything in *Kotlovan*, or to find a way to society in *Dzhan*. In his art the people are again and again portrayed as incapable of establishing a meaningful and dignified relationship with life and society; they fail, are cast off and wander about in alienation or confusion, unable to make sense of what they see and experience. It is in this manner that Platonov will seek to suggest the forgotten ways in which life after the Revolution signifies.

NOTES

1. On the relationship between Futurism and Proletkult in LEF, see for instance Kornienko (2010, 131f.).

2. Gorky regarded himself as a forerunner and teacher of the proletarian writer. He indefatigably wrote letters instructing writers or aspiring writers how to improve their works, and he authored several articles about how he learned to write and to write well.

3. For a discussion of the term, see Skakov (2014, 781), Borenstein (2000, 196–99), and Platt (1997, 144–59).

4. Almost ten years after Platonov wrote this response, Bataille developed his famous term "l'informe" (1929), which in English is translated in one dictionary as "formless." He concludes as follows: "affirming that the universe resembles nothing and is only formless amounts to saying that the universe is something like a spider or spit" (1985, 31). Undoubtedly, one can find similarities in the attempt of both writers to reach for the world beyond its classifications and in its insignificance and informal form. There are several points of intersection between the two communist authors. For instance, in relation to the notion of formlessness, we find the notion of the abject, and further, an interest in inner ecstasy. Yet there are certain fundamental differences that concern the understanding of the subject and sensitivity. Here the difference is most notably manifested in the word "spit" ("crachat"), which carries a provocative gesture that we do not find in the works of Platonov. Platonov's break with petty bourgeois taste involves a fundamental ethical concern for the significance of the formless and insignificant.

5. For Platonov at the time, "ekhidnyi" was a strongly negative word. See for instance "Zhivaia Ekhidna" in Platonov (2004, 37).

6. See further discussion of the feminine in the chapter about *Chevengur*.

7. References below to the story are by page number only.

8. A common trope in Platonov's world is that sleep both intensifies and exemplifies his characters' ways of being in the world.

9. See Meerson (1997).

10. The word "abject" is not intended here in either Kristeva's or Bataille's sense. Platonov attempts to approach the abject not as a position within a structural order, but as the possibility of retrieving forgotten meaning.

11. The story that most clearly illustrates this uncertainty is *Dzhan* (*Soul*), which is a tale about leaving the filth of poverty and entering—or really not entering—the forms of society.

12. Cf. Barthes (1953, 23f), who describes Socialist Realism as a system of values and significations.

13. Fredric Jameson (1994, 77), who approaches the question through Heidegger, insists that "In this society, therefore, in this history, all truths are also at one and the same time ideological, and should be celebrated with the greatest suspicion and vigilance."

TWO

Chevengur and the Movement
of the Revolution

Several years with several stories and essays pass between "Chuldik and Epishka" (1920) and the great novel *Chevengur* (1926–1928). Nevertheless, we can recognize in the later novel an aesthetics that can be characterized as formless, or rather, if we take the development of this aesthetics into account, as "headless." *Chevengur* is the longest and probably most disordered novel in Platonov's oeuvre, and this chaotic form reflects its theme—the Revolution and the utterly confused postrevolutionary time that it primarily chronicles. The novel begins in the early twentieth century but focuses on the Russian civil war during the first years after the Revolution, 1917–1923. It represents a conglomeration of several stories written at different times with different themes and without clear transitions between the different parts.[1] In this lack of a narrative line, we can discern a reflection of Platonov's endeavor to think about the nature and dynamics of the revolutionary transition from within its movement rather than from outside as a historical narrative. And he exposes to us a revolution that attempts to inscribe itself in history as a transcendent condition, an "after history," even though what it ought to be is the negation of the transcendent perspective of history. The subheading of the novel tells us that we will read a "journey with an open heart" ("puteshestvie s otkrytym serdtsem"), but although the movement of the main protagonists, Dvanov and Kopenkin, is dictated by their open heart, it does not take the form of a journey from one point to another, but can rather be likened to disoriented homeless wayfaring or roaming about. Thus, the two protagonists of the novel and the Revolution in the novel follow the movement of the Revolution in its implementation in the Russian countryside as its devoted, openhearted, and perturbed agents, and

33

in the midst of the dreadful consequences of this process they begin to
wonder, "Is this really socialism?" and "Where then is socialism?"

As Seifrid (1992, 104) remarks, the central structure of a journey, especially the journey of a young boy as he grows into a young man with a
revolutionary consciousness, is reminiscent of the *Bildungsroman*. In this
sense, the work has much in common with the structure of the Socialist
Realist novel, which, although it had not yet been introduced as the official doctrine of Soviet art, had already found a shape *avant la lettre* in the
later canonized novels of, for instance, Gladkov (1925/1926). It goes without saying, however, that *Chevengur* differs radically from the formation
of the revolutionary hero and his consciousness in these Socialist Realist
models, and one of the main reasons is Platonov's critique of the idea of
the formation of revolutionary awareness or consciousness.[2] The novel's
movement follows the chaos of the postrevolutionary calamities during
the Civil War as a reflection of the confusion in the minds of the recently
"liberated" or "emancipated" people of the Russian provinces. Here,
Platonov is beginning to find a form for his "inconspicuous paradoxicality" (Livingstone), the "ambivalence" (Seifrid) in his way of describing
from within how the quasi-rational, bureaucratic language of the revolutionary slogans destroy as they are implemented the experience of the
people that they really were aimed to enhance. This does not necessarily
mean that Platonov turns away from the revolutionary utopia of 1917 in
Chevengur, as has been asserted by scholars and critics, but it can be
argued that in this novel he has begun to depict post-Soviet society in the
double movement of the realization of the communist utopia.

Here the movement of the Revolution and history does not confirm
the Marxist dictum that revolutions are the locomotive of history, particularly not in the sense that it was interpreted in the Russian context as the
vehicle and motor of modernization. Moreover, instead of adhering to
the didactic Bolshevik program of "popular enlightenment" ("narodnoe
prosveshchenie") aimed at raising the people from their elementary and
spontaneous condition to the revolutionary awareness of new "revolutionary" subjects, Platonov attempts to grasp them in the dynamics of
their quest for consciousness, or their "spontaneous consciousness."[3] He
explores the Revolution as an ecstatic force looking for a head, or consciousness, that is constantly thrown back upon the formless or headless
qualities of its search. Moreover, the experience of headlessness is not
simply a theme, but also both an aesthetic antiaesthetic quality of the
narrative and a political antipolitical basis for the portrayal of utopia. The
characters of the novel enter the modern world attempting to "think with
their own heads" for the first time, but they appear to be "dubjects"
("dub'ekty") (Platonov 2009, 375) rather than the subjects or agents of the
Revolution, as Kopenkin puts it. The word *dubject* is a neologism that
Platonov invents by fusing the word for oak tree (*dub*), which colloquially
means "blockhead, numbskull" with "subject." The fact that Kopenkin

gets the word wrong confirms the claim and derides their failed attempts to acquire the new revolutionary dignity and subjectivity. Nothing in the novel is more dismal than their mistaken belief that they are implementing the Revolution by appropriating and carrying out the slogans.[4] And yet it is in the midst of these flawed historical interpretations from within a political language run amok as "spontaneous consciousness" that Platonov attempts to grasp another revolutionary experience of the world as a remembered dream on the boundary of the sort of consciousness possessed by people who lack a sense of being at home in the world and a subjectivity that allows them to inhabit that sense. As Günther (2011) and Seifrid (1992) have pointed out, the protagonists in the novel are depicted in their physicality because their body presents them with a different "consciousness," or rather, a different memory of an experience of themselves in the world in the midst of their errings and wanderings dictated by revolutionary slogans.

In its ruminations on the dynamics of revolutionary consciousness, *Chevengur* becomes not solely an answer to the Revolution but also a unique modernist attempt to deal with the problem of subjectivity in the modern novel. The Hungarian Marxist literary theoretician Georg Lukács called this the "problem of the transcendental locus,"[5] which is how he defines the problem of the subjective consciousness in a world that lacks an absolute transcendental perspective. In his exposé of the form principle of the modern novel, Lukács distinguishes within the *Bildungsroman* a "problem" or problematic feature, namely that it constantly portrays "the deep perplexity of life," ("die tiefe Ratlosigkeit des Lebens").[6] Thus, according to the literary theoretician, the novel expresses the "transcendental homelessness" of the modern world, the fact that man is left to himself to discover meaning in a world that does not speak of meaning on its own. The subject of the novel does not live in accordance with the world of transcendental meaning; he must always make a journey towards himself to reach a "recognition of himself," if only in the form of "a glimpse of meaning."[7] If Lukács laments the preoccupation with the position of the subject in what appears as a lack of a totality of being in a world abandoned by God, he nevertheless pinpoints a substantial aspect of the modern novel—the problematic question of the acquisition of knowledge and awareness in the formation of the subject with respect to the sociohistorical situation. This same theme appears as a problem in Platonov's works as well, particularly in *Chevengur*. Instead of lamenting transcendence, however, the Soviet writer radicalizes the modern novel with respect to precisely this lack.[8] The absence of a transcendent perspective is the starting point of the novel and, to a certain extent, the theme that determines its movement. Although the characters constantly discuss the meaning of the Revolution, none of them offers any insights from which we can read any moral to the story, and Platonov does not introduce any subject who seeks to resolve this meaninglessness by finding or offering a meaning. The headless or asubjective movement of the Revolution is to a certain degree its truth, but we cannot establish the meaning of this truth except in the retrieval of the utopia of what is forgotten or lost in that world.[9]

The relation to transcendent reason determines Platonov's understanding of the problems of the implementation of the Revolution as well as his understanding of its inconspicuous movement. If the Revolution appears as the idea that transcendent reason has already been attained, in *Chevengur,* Platonov instead abandons the attempt to get a glimpse into a transcendental point of experience in subjectivity, thereby relinquishing the notion itself of such an experience.

In his particular form of narrative, both the narrator and the main character—the writer's typical alter ego—follow the movements of the revolutionary world as ecstatic whims as they discover the way in which reality speaks through its meaningless attempts to establish meaning. Indeed, the lack or loss of a subjective perspective on existence does not appear as a tragic point that can find resolution in the life of the hero; instead, it offers itself as the necessary condition for experiencing common life. Living without insight or any sense of orientation and righteousness is the point from which the Revolution begins in *Chevengur.* It also marks the beginning of Platonov's writing of the Revolution, which takes the form of a reading of a world that lacks a transcendental point from which to look back at it, and an exploration of other ways in which the world and the Revolution speak through different ways of experiencing the world, such as in dreams or in other semiconscious conditions or in the body.

IN BETWEEN LIFE AND DEATH

The first part of the novel was originally written as a story entitled "Origin of a Master" ("Proiskhozdenie mastera"), about the early life and upbringing of the young boy Aleksandr (Sasha) Dvanov. The novel begins on the boundary between the inhabited world and nature, at the now famous "vetkhie opushki,"[10] which translates as "ancient outskirts" or "tumbledown outskirts."[11] Platonov, who is a master at conjoining transferred and concrete meaning, evokes both notions to convey the image of a separate locus in close proximity to nature and death, which is abandoned because it is ancient, and ancient because it is abandoned. These outskirts are a locus on the borders of civilization, where people live a nearly nonalienated life and the difference between life and death is not so sharp. The first character that we meet, Zakhar Pavlovich, is the only paternal figure in the novel: he is to become the foster father of the main protagonist, Sasha Dvanov. He is described as a craftsman, and as almost the perfect image of a man whose relation to his work and life is nonreified according to Marx's theory of alienation. The first scene relates the death of Zakhar Pavlovich's friend, simply called "a hermit" or "a loner" ("bobyl'"), and Zakhar Pavlovich consoles him: "'Don't be afraid,'" Zakhar Pavlovich answered positively. "I'd die right now myself, but, you know how it is, when you are working on different things'" (20) ("Ne boisia, - polozhitel'no otvetil Zakhar Pavlovich. – Ia by sam khot' seichas umer, da vse, znaesh, zanimaeshsia raznymi izdeliami") (14). The crafts-man relates to the world as it appears to him or calls upon him out of necessity. He never refuses to "fix or equip" anything, but he has no personal interest in the world and no interest in his own person. Instead he lives with an "indifferent tenderness" (3). As a parallel to him, the loner has also lived his entire life amazed and startled, "not at all afflicted by life" (4) ("sovsem ne oderzhim zhizniiu") (12). The Russian expres-sion, "oderzhim zhizniiu," is stronger than in the translation "afflicted by life," and can also be rendered as "possessed by" or "obsessed with" life. In other words, the loner appears as a person akin to Zakhar Pavlovich, who is not possessed by his personal interests in life, and indeed not by life itself either. Their puritanism is also what makes them open to the world.

This indifferent kinship with life and death appears as a positive qual-ity of Zakhar Pavlovich and later of Sasha Dvanov in a way that is remi-niscent of Gerasim in Tolstoy's *The Death of Ivan Ilyich*. It bespeaks the experience of the world in an in-between of life and death which keeps them from the erring forms of personal or historical self-manifestation and self-interest in which the other characters become caught up. The hermit, for instance, lives in wonder of the world, waiting for it to be explained and for the general fuss to come to an end. His experience of the world is not "transformed," but appears to him in a fusion of concrete and metaphorical meaning. This is for instance the case in the following dialogue, when Zakhar Pavlovich attempts to explain to him why the wind blows:

> In fact, when Zakhar Pavlovich tried to tell him why the wind blows, instead of standing in one place, the hermit was even more amazed and understood nothing, even though he accurately felt the wind coming up.
> "No, really? Tell me, tell me. . . . The sun's overcooking, must be? A pretty business!"
> Zakhar Pavlovich explained that overcooking was not a pretty busi-ness, but simply heat.
> "Heat?!" The hermit was astounded. "Says, you, you witch!"
> The recluse's amazement only hopped from one thing to another, but nothing in his consciousness was transformed. Instead of a mind, he lived with a feeling of trusting respect. (4f)

[Действительно, когда Захар Павлович попробовал ему рассказать, отчего ветер дует, а не стоит на месте, бобыль еще более удивился и ничего не понимал, хотя чувствовал происхождение ветра точно.

— Да неужто? Скажи пожалуйста! Стало быть, от солнечного припеку? Милое дело!

Захар Павлович объяснил, что припек дело не милое, а просто жара.

— Жара?! — удивился бобыль. — Ишь ты, ведьма какая!

У бобыля только передвигалось удивление с одной вещи на другую, но в сознание ничего не превращалось. Вместо ума он жил чувством доверчивого уважения] (13)

The hermit is portrayed somewhat condescendingly, and yet there is something ideal in the way he experiences the world in "trusting respect"—that is, as something kindred and intimate, and not as an object to be transformed according to the categories of knowledge. His ability to live in apprehension of an explanation of life appears equally as an ability to live without this explanation, which can be contrasted with the desire for the attainment of a transcendent reason in Communism. The notion of transcendent knowledge and indifference is further developed in the parable-like story of the death of Sasha Dvanov's father, which also appears at the very beginning of the book. He was a fisherman who died when he jumped into Lake Mutevo in order to find out the "secret of death":

Zakhar Pavlovich had known one man, a fisherman from Lake Mutevo, who had questioned many people about death and whose curiosity had filled him with *toska*; this fisherman had loved fish not as food but as special beings that definitely knew the secret of death. He would show Zakhar Pavlovich the eyes of dead fish and say, "Look—there's wisdom! A fish stands between life and death, so that he's dumb and without expression. I mean even a calf thinks, but a fish no. It already knows everything." Contemplating the lake through the years, the fisherman thought always about the same thing: about the interest of death. Zakhar Pavlovich tried to talk him out of it: "There's nothing special there—just something tight." After a year, the fisherman couldn't stand it any more and threw himself into the lake from his boat, after tying his feet with a rope so that he wouldn't accidentally float. In secret he did not even believe in death. The important thing was that he wanted to look what was there: perhaps it was more interesting than living in a village or on the shores of a lake. He saw death as another province, located under the heavens, as if at the bottom of cool water, and it attracted him. . . . Dmitry Ivanich tried: three days later he was dragged out of the lake and buried by the fence in the village churchyard. (21)

[Захар Павлович знал одного человека, рыбака с озера Мутево, который многих расспрашивал о смерти и тосковал от своего любопытства; этот рыбак больше всего любил рыбу, не как пищу, а как особое существо, наверное знающее тайну смерти. Он

показывал глаза мертвых рыб Захару Павловичу и говорил: "Гляди
— премудрость. Рыба между жизнью и смертью стоит, оттого она
и немая и глядит без выражения; телок ведь и тот думает, а рыба
нет — она все уже знает." Созерцая озеро годами, рыбак думал все
об одном и том же — об интересе смерти. Захар Павлович его
отговаривал: "Нет там ничего особого: так, что-нибудь тесное."
Через год рыбак не вытерпел и бросился с лодки в озеро, связав
себе ноги веревкой, чтобы нечаянно не поплыть. Втайне он вообще
не верил в смерть, главное, же, он хотел посмотреть — что там есть:
может быть, гораздо интересней, чем жить в селе или на
берегуозера; он видел смерть как другую губернию, которая
расположена под небом, будто на дне прохладной воды, — и она
его влекла. Некоторые мужики, которым рыбак говорил о своем
намерении пожить в смерти и вернуться, отговаривали его, а
другие соглашались с ним: "Что ж, испыток не убыток, Митрий
Иваныч. Пробуй, потом нам расскажешь." Дмитрий Иванович
попробовал: его вытащили из озера через трое суток и
похоронили у ограды на сельском погосте.] (15f)

The story of the fisherman, which may seem fantastic and absurd
owing to its fairytale-like qualities, in some respects seems to encapsulate
the story of *Chevengur*, which is also the story of the Revolution. Because
it is fantastic, however, it marks a nonentry that announces the impossibility of attaining transcendence and knowledge. The fish's indifference
and lack of expression is to the fisherman a token of "true wisdom," a
sign that it "knows everything already," including "the secret of death."
He therefore throws himself into the water, "after tying his feet," and
dies. If he did discover "the secret of death," he took it with him. The
point of this truism is to establish the opposite of a consciousness at work
in being. What the fish knows is knowledge that haunts the imagination
of the fisherman and Communism as "another province" that we would
like to enter. In other words, in this passage death presents itself to the
fisherman as a transcendent realm, and the failure to reach it in life is
suggestive also of the problem of the Revolution. As we learn later in the
chapter about the city of Chevengur, neither the communist leader nor
the fisherman could bear the "mystery of time" or "the mystery of life"
(318), and both of them therefore attempted to cut short the road to the
otherworldly. I will return to this passage further ahead. The problem is
not so much the imagination of Communism or of death, but the attempt
to realize or attain this imagination in time.

Platonov renders and illustrates this imaginational power through *erlebte Rede*, that is, free indirect speech, which, as Robert Hodel (2001) has
shown, became a characteristic device in his work. At first the story of the
fisherman is a straightforward narrative interspersed with direct speech,
but then it shifts to the indirect mode. For instance, this: "The important
thing was that he wanted to look what was there: perhaps it was more
interesting than living in a village or on the shores of a lake." Platonov

uses *erlebte Rede* like this to enter into or represent the imagination of the character in its dialogicity, that is, in the way that within the character, the inner and outer world and inner and outer speech are for the most part indistinguishable from each other. In other words, there is a parallel between the realm of death as the locus of the indifferent and indistinguishable and the revolutionary utopia striving to encompass the entire world in its appearance beyond the categories of desire, consciousness, and evaluation. As the story of the fisherman suggests, however, life cannot be excluded from this utopia of the nondifferentiated. Platonov therefore seeks to represent the world on the very border of differentiation and indifferentiation.

Thus, the locus of death plays a central role and will represent a sort of homeless home for Sasha. The tale of the fisherman's death in the lake forms a circular story bounded by his father's death and his own demise. The novel ends when the communist city of Chevengur has finally perished and Aleksandr dives into the lake to be reunited with his father. The structure of the work underscores the notion that life is a rather aimless in-between movement, and that its explanations of the world cannot cut short the mysteries of its time. The novel takes place in between these deaths, portraying how the fatherless Aleksandr wanders about the world first as a homeless orphan and then as a revolutionary child without any clear aim except his indistinct search for a home and an equally vague search for socialism. He is at first taken up and adopted by the poor Dvanov family, whose name he is to carry as a sign of his alienation from his identity. Sasha arrives in his new family without any possessions, and he will remain destitute throughout the entire novel. When the Dvanovs cannot offer him a home they drive him away, and he heads to the graveyard where his father is buried—the only place that offers him a sense of a home and a sense of self:

> Sasha went into the graveyard, not recognizing what he wanted to do. For the first time he thought now about himself and touched his chest. Here I am, and all around everything was foreign, unlike himself. The house in which he had lived, had loved Prokhor Abramovich, Mavra Fetisovna and Proshka, turned out not to be his house. He had been lead out of it onto the cold road in the morning. In his half-childish saddened soul, undiluted by the comforting water of consciousness, was clenched a full crushing insult, which he felt up into his throat. (18f)

> [Саша вошел на кладбище не сознавая, чего ему хочется. В первый раз он подумал сейчас про себя и тронул свою грудь: вот тут я, — а всюду было чужое и непохожее на него. Дом, в котором он жил, где любил Прохора Абрамовича, Мавру Фетисовну и Прошку, оказался не его домом — его вывели оттуда утром на прохладную дорогу. В полудетской грустной душе, не разбавленной

успокаивающей водой сознания, сжалась полная давящая обида — он чувствовал ее до горла.] (31)

Sasha comes to a kind of semiawareness that he is nowhere at home and nowhere himself except in this graveyard, where he thinks, "Here I am," or rather, "This is where I am." His existence in proximity to nonbeing is closely related to the nearly asubjective anonymity suggested by his lack of a name. Moreover, just as he lives in a kind of in-between with no proper name himself, he also develops a sensibility to the world as a nameless in-between. When he becomes a student, he reads the world as follows:

> No matter how much he read and thought, some kind of hollow place remained ever within him, an emptiness through which an undescribed and untold world passed like a startled wind. At seventeen Dvanov still had no armor over his heart, neither belief in God nor any other intellectual comfort. He did not give a stranger's name to the nameless life which opened before him. However, he did not want that world to remain untitled; he only waited to hear its own proper name, instead of a purposely conceived appellation. (43)

> [Сколько он ни читал и ни думал, всегда у него внутри оставалось какое-то порожнее место — та пустота, сквозь которую тревожным ветром проходит неописанный и нерассказанный мир. В семнадцать лет Дванов еще не имел брони над сердцем — ни веры в бога, ни другого умственного покоя; он не давал чужого имени открывающейся перед ним безымянной жизни. Однако он не хотел, чтобы мир оставался ненареченным, — он только ожидал услышать его собственное имя из его же уст, вместо нарочно выдуманных прозваний.] (60)

Dvanov carries within him "a hollow place," or emptiness, which makes him receptive to the world as a natural phenomenon within him. Here we find an exquisite example of Platonov's attempt to co-mingle concrete and metaphorical meanings so as to undo the alleged metaphysical distinction between concrete meaning and metaphor. The words "hollow place" ("porozhnee mesto") and "emptiness" ("pustota"), as the "startled wind" can undoubtedly also be read as metaphors and images of his spiritual or mental receptiveness and ability to wonder as he confronts the experience of an unnamed world. Potentially, however, the passage can be read as a fusion of the metaphorical and concrete level in the experience of "existential matter" (*veshchestvo sushchestvovaniia*). This will be all the more apparent in the notion that he heeds the world in order to "hear its own proper name" from "its own lips," ("iz ego zhe ust"). Here Platonov defies the Romantic poetics of the ineffable in favor of a quest for a world that speaks in its own name. We are in addition offered an explanation of the subtitle "a journey with an open heart," because it is this odyssey that leads Dvanov into the revolutionary movement, and it is also this quest that appears to be at stake in the Revolution. Emptiness in an open heart is moreover the "origin of a Master."

THE REVOLUTION

Although the movement of the Revolution is the main theme of the novel, and really also a central theme throughout Platonov's works, the event itself takes up remarkably little space. The revolutionary year from February to October 1917 is described in less than a page. And the Revolution is told not as a historical occurrence or objective fact, but as certain distant calamities filtered through the skeptical minds and laconic conversations of Zakhar Pavlovich and his wife:

> Disillusioned by old age and the lost wanderings of his entire life, he was not at all surprised by the revolution.
>
> "Revolution is easier than war," he explained to Sasha. "People won't do for a difficult business, something's not quite right. . . ."
>
> Now it was impossible to deceive Zakhar Pavlovich, and for the sake of being unmistaken, he rejected the revolution.
>
> He told all the workers that the smartest people were again on duty in the government so no good could come of it.
>
> He made fun of it right up until October, feeling for the first time the satisfaction of being an intelligent man. However, one October night he heard shooting in the city and spent the entire night outside, only coming into the hut to light his cigarettes. All night long he was slamming doors, not letting his wife sleep.
>
> "Settle down already, you mad dog!" the old woman tossed about in solitude. "A pedestrian, a true pedestrian! And what'll come now? No bread, no clothes! How is it their hands don't wither from shooting? It's clear they grew up without mothers!"
>
> Zakhar Pavlovich stood in the yard with a smoldering cigarette, nodding at the distant shooting.
>
> "Can it really be so?" Zakhar Pavlovich would ask himself and then go into the hut to light a new cigarette.
>
> "Lie down, demon!" his wife advised him. "Sasha, you asleep?" Zakhar Pavlovich was excited. "The idiots there are taking the power, but maybe life will get smarter." (59)

[Разочарованный старостью и заблуждениями всей своей жизни, он ничуть не удивился революции.

— Революция легче, чем война, — объяснял он Саше. На трудное дело люди не пойдут: тут что-нибудь не так . . .

Теперь Захара Павловича невозможно было обмануть, и он, ради безошибочности, отверг революцию.

Он всем мастеровым говорил, что у власти опять умнейшие люди дежурят — добра не будет.

До самого октября месяца он насмехался, в первый раз почувствовав удовольствие быть умным человеком. Но в одну

октябрьскую ночь он услышал стрельбу в городе и всю ночь
пробыл на дворе, заходя в горницу лишь закурить. Всю ночь он
хлопал дверями, не давая заснуть жене.

— Да угомонись ты, идол бешеный! — ворочалась в
одиночестве старуха. Вот пешеход-то! И что теперь будет ни хлеба,
ни одежи! Как у них руки-то стрелять не отсохнут без матерей,
видно, росли!

Захар Павлович стоял посреди двора с пылающей цигаркой,
поддакивая дальней стрельбе.

"Неужели это так?" — спрашивал себя Захар Павлович и
уходил закуривать новую цигарку.

— Ложись, леший! — советовала жена.

— Саша, ты не спишь? — волновался Захар Павлович. Там
дураки власть берут, — может, хоть жизнь поумнеет.] (62)

Such a conversation would of course have been impossible in a Socialist Realist novel. It is nevertheless typical of *Chevengur* and illustrates
how the novel renders the Revolution as an event that is not retold but
interpreted through the understanding of the people of the province.
Initially they appear to regard the revolutionary year of 1917 with disap-
proval and suspicion, but their attitudes will be varied and highly ambiv-
alent. Zakhar Pavlovich, for instance, thinks that "something's not quite
right," and it is even told that "for the sake of being unmistaken, he
rejected the Revolution," and his wife cries out, "And what'll come now?
No bread, no clothes!" That is, she sees the Revolution as leading only to
starvation, which, as Platonov of course knew as he wrote *Chevengur*, it
really did. Ultimately, Zakhar Pavlovich exclaims, "The idiots there are
taking power, perhaps life will get smarter!" However, this is not the last
word about the Revolution on the part of its heroes or the writer.

Thus, in a remarkable way, Platonov portrays the Revolution not as a
glorious, heroic event, but as the question of a legacy, which not only can
be interpreted in different ways but is also experienced by the people and
lives in them in different ways. The next morning, Sasha and Zakhar
Pavlovich go to town to register in a party, and as they debate with the
representatives of various groups, different facets and interpretations of
its meaning come into play. In the end, and despite a conversation in
which Zakhar Pavlovich discloses that what the party representative says
is idle newspaper talk, they nevertheless decide to register with the
Bolsheviks. The reason, we learn, is as follows:

"Sash," he said, "you're an orphan, you got your life cheap. Don't be
stingy with it, live the main life." . . .

"So they're Bolsheviks and high martyrs to their idea," Zakhar Pavlovich was making a hash of everything "but you look it over real
careful. Remember—your father drowned, Lord knows who your
mother was, millions of people are living without souls . . . that's a

great cause . . . a Bolshevik has to have an empty heart, so he can make room in it for everything." (47)

[— Саш, — сказал он, — ты сирота, тебе жизнь досталась задаром. Не жалей ее, живи главной жизнью. . .

— Хоть они и большевики и великомученики своей идеи, — напутствовал Захар Павлович, — но тебе надо глядеть и глядеть. Помни — у тебя отец утонул, мать неизвестно кто, миллионы людей без души живут, — тут великое дело . . . Большевик должен иметь пустое сердце, чтобы туда все могло поместиться.] (66)

The Revolution, which stands out as a catastrophic muddle of bureaucratic false assertions about the people and power, is at the same time promises the possibility to life "the main life" without sparing it; it is the promise of an empty heart, so that there can be "room in it for everything." This suggests how Sasha and other heroes in later novels will carry the Revolution within them—as an empty room and an open heart, as opposed to the confused language of party propaganda. It is also, however, a strange promise of death. When after the Revolution he and Zakhar Pavlovich go around asking different political parties about their ideas and programs, the Socialists declare

that man is such a splendid and avaricious being, that it is even strange to think about the satiation of his happiness, which would have been the end of the world. (60)

[что человек настолько великолепное и жадное существо, что даже странно думать о насыщении его счастьем — это был бы конец света.] (63)

If the Revolution (and modern society) promise complete happiness, the pledge that attracts Zakhar Pavlovich and Aleksandr is the idea that it will lead to "the end of the world." The notion refers to the Marxist concept of the end of history, but filtered through the provincial party representatives, it acquires a very special meaning for Aleksandr. He understands the promised land of the Revolution as the end of the world—the world where the secret of death will be revealed to his father:

Alexander wasn't offended. He felt Zakhar Pavlovich's sincere need, but he believed that the revolution was the end of the world. In the future world, though, Zakhar Pavlovich's alarm would be instantaneously destroyed and his fisherman father would find that for the sake of which he had voluntarily drowned himself. In his own clear feeling Alexander already had that new world, but he could only make it, not recount it. (48)

[Александр не обижался. Он чувствовал сердечную жажду Захара Павловича, но верил, что революция — это конец света. В будущем же мире мгновенно уничтожится тревога Захара Павловича, а отец-рыбак найдет то, ради чего он своевольно утонул. В своем ясном чувстве Александр уже имел тот новый свет, но его можно лишь сделать, а не рассказать.] (61)

The notion that "the revolution was the end of the world" acquires an ambiguous meaning, considering that it will ultimately appear almost as Armageddon in *Chevengur*. The combination of the themes of fatherlessness and "apocalypticism" (Bethea 1989, 147), have been interpreted several times against the backdrop of the works of Nikolay Fedorov (Bethea 1989; Geller 1982; Mörch 1998). However, there seems be a suggestion of another thanatology than that of Fedorov here. The "end of the world" as the beginning of "that new world" can also be read as Platonov's particular way of existentializing Fedorov's inspiration. Repeatedly, Platonov returns to the idea that the world will speak of itself in its entirety and kinship in the emptiness of an open heart, or in experiences of the inner self on the boundary of death. This is the case, for instance, when after having joined the Red Army in the civil war, Sasha meets a soldier who implores him to close his eyes:

> "Close my sight for me!" and glanced at him with drying, unblinking eyeballs, without the slightest tremor of his lids.
>   "How come?" Dvanov asked, growing upset with shame.
>   "It cuts . . . " the Red soldier explained, and clenched his teeth so as to shut his eyes. The eyes however, would not close; rather they burned and bloomed, turning into globular mineral. The reflection of the cloudy sky came vividly into his dead eyes, as though nature returned into a person as the life which had opposed it head-on left, and the Red soldier, in order not to torment himself, accustomed himself to it with death. (56)

> [— Закрой мне зрение! — и глядел, не моргая, засыхающими глазами, без всякой дрожи век.
>   — А что? — спросил Александр и забеспокоился от стыда.
>   — Режет . . . — объяснил красноармеец и сжал зубы, чтобы закрыть глаза. Но глаза не закрывались, а выгорали и выцветали, превращаясь в мутный минерал. В его умерших глазах явственно прошли отражения облачного неба — как будто природа возвратилась в человека после мешавшей ей встречной жизни, и красноармеец, чтобы не мучиться, приспособился к ней смертью.] (76f)

In the image of the dying soldier, Platonov rewrites in an unusual manner the common custom of closing the eyes of a dead person. The dying person asks him to "close his sight" because the sight hurts him; it "cuts." When Dvanov does not do this, the eyes of the dying man instead come to reflect the sky, the world, and nature in a nonseeing manner: "as though nature returned into a person as the life which had opposed it head-on left." There is in other words a kind of asubjective nonseeing on the border between life and death; the world is not seen by someone, but is instead presented as being in that person. Here there is also a hint of Platonov's nonseeing realism. Obviously, to reflect the world as it is was one of the main aesthetic aspirations of modern realism—we can need only think of Stendhal's mirror. What is reflected here, however, not, as realism insists, an outside world in a consciousness or in a form of writing. What is instead reflected and retold is a seeing (Dvanov's) of the nonseeing of the dying soldier, and this nonseeing encloses the world in itself on the border of death. Moreover, Platonov asserts that the dying soldier can reflect and be this world in himself because his own life, which is now leaving him, no longer opposes this world "head-on." In other words, on the boundary of death, life, as opposed to the world perceived through the *principium indivuationis*, is challenged and the world is remembered in the Inner.

THE "EUNUCH OF THE SOUL"

After joining the Red Army, Sasha follows the movement of the Revolution as it takes him back and forth across the Russian countryside. Here the narrative becomes utterly confused and we meet him in different forms of "doing" the Revolution in the war, and in his scattered meetings with different persons who each in their way attempt to survive in the new world. Dvanov is at one point called a "subject-man" ("sub'ekt-chelovek" [86]), because he is not simply acting out of necessity. Yet it is precisely his lack of subjectivity and individuation that forms his relation to the world. He is characterized at the age of sixteen as "having no aims" and in the power of "outer visions," much as travelers are possessed by what they see in new countries ("Im vladeli vneshnie videniia, kak vladeiut svezhie strany puteshestvennikom") (55). When we meet him in a half-conscious state after being injured in the civil war, he is only more exposed to a world in which there is no sense of orientation:

> Dvanov began to toss restlessly. He had frightened himself in a dream, thinking that his heart was stopping, and he sat on the floor as he woke up. "But where then is socialism?" Dvanov remembered, and peered into the room, searching for this thing. It seemed to him that he had already found it, but then wasted it in his sleep among these strangers. Dvanov went out in fear of the punishment to come, hatless and in his socks, saw the dangerous unanswering night and dashed off to the village into his own distance. (94)

> [Дванов заметался в беспокойстве — он испугался во сне, что у него останавливается сердце, и сел на полу в пробуждении. — А где же социализм-то? вспомнил Дванов и поглядел в тьму комнаты, ища свою вещь; ему редставилось, что он его уже нашел, но утратил во сне среди этих чужих людей. В испуге будущего наказания Дванов

без шапки и в чулках вышел наружу, увидел опасную, безответную
ночь и побежал через деревню в свою даль.] (103)

Jameson (1994, 95) maintains à propos this paragraph that *Chevengur*
portrays the "fascinating inner psychology of the Utopian process." Indeed, what is interesting in the novel are not only the inner workings of
utopia, but also how Platonov explores what utopian dynamics can tell
us about consciousness and inner psychology. Political utopia is dependent on its realization, on a place where it has become real, but in the
novel utopia is for the most part at work in sleep, in dreams and in the
memory of what has been forgotten. According to one of the songs that
the soldiers sing, it is that distant dream which has fallen into the hands
of the enemy:

> *On the far shore of the deep*
> *Lies in that far distant land*
> *What we but dream in our sleep*
> *And our foe holds in his hand. . . . (70)*

> [Есть в далекой стране,
> На другом берегу,
> Что нам снится во сне,
> Но досталось врагу . . .] (93)

The song continues as a folkloric fairy tale about an apple that symbolizes
the utopia of the Revolution with all its hopes, and it ends on the rather
anarchistic note that it must not bring fruit "for soviets, not for tsars,/ But
for all mankind!" (70) The opposition in the novel between the party and
the people is not as straightforward as the song heralds, and there we
will find official revolutionaries who somehow seem to carry that distant
dream within them too. Yet the song brings us an image of a revolutionary promise as a dream, whose realization seems to have fallen into the
wrong hands. The result is an inversion of the very notion of the locus of
utopia and the importance of consciousness: utopia in *Chevengur* is true
not in its realization but in its inner psychology. Thus, Dvanov's half-
conscious condition is presented as but one state among others in a world
that offers no answers or realization. Socialism appears as a beckoning
point of orientation that he had found, "but had lost in his sleep" in a
world that is dangerous and "unanswering" ("bezotvetnaia"). He therefore runs to "into his own distance" or into "his own open spaces" ("v
svoiu dal'"). Possessing nothing, Dvanov moves continuously into a distant, open, mute world, guided only by the memory of a lost vision.[12]

Dvanov's different conditions constitute his being in the world, but
they do not affect either his judgements or his activity.[13] He can disappear to himself or forget himself and end up in places for no other reason
than the whims of events. It is telling that Platonov addresses the question of consciousness in an extensive passage a bit farther on, in the

image of Sasha as guarded only by the "eunuch of the soul." This "eunuch" really presents an image of man's awareness or consciousness as something isolated from him, because he is not in possession of a home or at home in himself. The eunuch is our guardian observer, but we have no access to him:

Two days later Aleksandr remembered why he lived and where he had been sent. But there is within man also a tiny spectator who takes part neither in action nor in suffering, who is always cold-blooded and the same. It is his service to see and be a witness, but he is without franchise in the life of man and it is not known why he exists in solitude. This corner of a man's consciousness is lit both day and night like the doorman's room in a large building. This heart[14] doorman sits entire days at the entrance into man and knows all the inhabitants of this building, but not a single resident asks the doorman's advice about his affairs. The tenants come and go; while the spectator-doorman watches them with his eyes. His powerless knowledge of everything makes him sometimes seem sad, but he is always polite, distant, and he keeps an apartment in another building. In the event of fire the doorman telephones the firemen and watches further events from without.

While Dvanov walked and road without memory, this spectator within him saw everything, but it never warned or helped him. He lived parallel to Dvanov, but he wasn't Dvanov.

He existed somewhat like a man's dead brother; everything human seemed to be at hand, but something tiny and vital was missing. Man never remembers him, but always trusts him; in the same way, just as when a tenant leaves his house and his wife within, he is never jealous of her and the doorman.

This is the eunuch of man's soul. It was to this he was a witness. (79f)

[Через два дня Александр вспомнил, зачем он живет и куда послан. Но в человеке еще живет маленький зритель — он не участвует ни в поступках, ни в страдании — он всегда хладнокровен и одинаков. Его служба — это видеть и быть свидетелем, но он без права голоса в жизни человека и неизвестно, зачем он одиноко существует. Этот угол сознания человека день и ночь освещен, как комната швейцара в большом доме. Круглые сутки сидит этот бодрствующий швейцар в подъезде человека, знает всех жителей своего дома, но ни один житель не советуется со швейцаром о своих делах. Жители входят и выходят, а зритель-швейцар провожает их глазами. От своей бессильной осведомленности он кажется иногда печальным, но всегда вежлив, уединен и имеет квартиру в другом доме. В случае пожара швейцар звонит пожарным и наблюдает снаружи дальнейшие события.

Пока Дванов в беспамятстве ехал и шел, этот зритель в нем все видел, хотя ни разу не предупредил и не помог. Он жил параллельно Дванову, но Двановым не был.

Он существовал как бы мертвым братом человека: в нем все человеческое имелось налицо, но чего-то малого и главного недоставало. Человек никогда не помнит его, но всегда ему доверяется — так житель, уходя из дома и оставляя жену, никогда не ревнует к ней швейцара.

Это евнух души человека. Вот чему он был свидетелем.] (104)

The image of the eunuch of the soul has been interpreted several times with reference to the theme of castration and Platonov's complex relationship with sexuality, which is also reflected in Dvanov's rather asexual love in the novel.[15] Indeed, it gives us a perspective from which we can approach Platonov's puritanism (Borenstein 2000), his critique of bourgeois culture as the "passion for/of sex" ("strastiu pola") in his early works in terms of the "inadmissibility of desire" (Naiman 1988). For Platonov, the utopia of Communism and the consummation of desire offer two competing experiences of communality in the Inner and in intimacy. If Communism meant the possibility of retrieving a bond to the common world or common existence as it lives in us beyond conscious relations, he discards the notion of a Communism based on desire (as, for instance, according to Bataille), because like Hegel before him, he understands desire as linked to self-consciousness.[16] According to the Oxford Dictionary, the eunuch is "a man who has been castrated, especially (in the past) one employed to guard the women's living areas at an oriental court." More important in Platonov's description of the eunuch, however, are the notions of man's impotence and isolation with regard to the domesticity of his Inner—that is, his ego or consciousness. The eunuch is not a metaphor for the human soul as a castrated and disinterested higher being, but an image of the way that man in his Inner is not his consciousness, not at home in himself. The eunuch of the soul is "a corner of man's consciousness," an isolated spectator that lives in man and sees everything but cannot communicate anything to him because man lives for the most part ecstatically, outside of himself. Indeed, Platonov's metaphor of the eunuch presents an image of man's Inner as a building with several inhabitants ("zhiteli"). People walk in and out of the self, and there is only this "ever-vigilant" doorman who stands for continuity and consistency. He is what is always present yet constantly absent, has no say in the life that he observes, and doesn't even live in man—he has a "room in another building." Not even at times when one would think that the person that he guards needs him the most—not even in "the event of fire," that is, at moments of danger or other harrowing experiences, is he present.

The presence of such a corner in man's consciousness is linked to an intimacy in the self where there is a lack of desire—the eunuch is the guardian of the intimate self. He appears to be what we would understand as awareness or an "objective," disinterested consciousness that registers the world as it is. But this consciousness of the world is not given to man, for he is a "dead brother" even to man himself, and, as mentioned, it is in moments bordering on death that he can attain the world in himself. Platonov points to a moment of loss or becoming the other in desire which Heidegger would term *Verfallenheit*; that is, fallenness in the fact of being in a *there*, a *da*—in the ex-, outside of the self. For Platonov, however, this is the truth about the ego—the self is really never at home in itself, not its own onlooker, because existence is temporal and ecstatic, and the Inner is not primarily an intimacy with the self or with the beloved; it is the others as they walk in and out of us in the form of existential impressions, or rather, in the form of ourselves. Thus, Platonov also conveys the notion that inwardly man is always other to himself as well, be it at a moment of desire or a moment of vigilance. Consciousness, or observation, lives in man detached from him; and life in the common world, or rather life as the common world, is true to itself in its moments of heedlessness and alienation.

THE "DUBJECT" OF THE REVOLUTION AND SHARED LIFE

Because there is no continuous and consistent subject to reflect the world in the novel, we encounter instead characters who are always in the midst of trying to find a meaning for their new existence after the Revolution. They lack not only homes but also the subjectivity needed to desire a home. Here between the classical novel that Lukács describes in the *Theory of the Novel* and Platonov's *Chevengur*, we see a decisive difference as to the nature of the literary subject, its agency, and the forms in which an understanding of the world can be attained. At stake in the *Theory of the Novel* is the status of the subject as an "onlooker" who can understand and relate to the world as a literary subject. There, moments of seclusion are moments of epiphany. By contrast, in *Chevengur*, the characters are exposed to us in their inability to grasp the world, and although they seek to form a relationship with reality, there is no transcendental gaze that can gauge their endeavors, and there are no moments of seclusion. Moreover, the absence of a transcendental position for the subject in the novel also reflects the lack of a transcendental position for the writing subject. There appears to be almost no direction in the narrative, which, just like the characters, is driven both from the inside and the outside by the whimsical logic of events.

Platonov's narrative style in *Chevengur* has been likened to the Russian fairy tale, neoprimitivism, and absurdism.(Hansen-Löwe 2012). On his road, Dvanov meets not only the girl, Sonya Aleksandrova Mandrova, whose name and timid character remind us of the heroine Sonya Marmeladova in *Crime and Punishment*, but also a person who calls himself Dostoyevsky, and one who is called "god" because gets all his nutrition only from the soil. The absurdism of the narrative, however, appears to be not so much a stylistic device as an attempt to capture the absurd fusion of different layers of culture and different orientations and disorientations of the world. Here, as mentioned, is a transposed realism aimed at showing how the world lives in us, and how it lives us. Moreover, *Chevengur* seems to contain a strange apologia for Don Quixote, in the sense that it seems to say to us that the hidalgo is right to joust with the windmills and correct in the errors he commits in service of the world.

Convinced that Communism is the foremost cause in the postrevolutionary world, Sasha goes into the steppe, where he fights in the civil war. There he meets his comrade-in-arms, Kopenkin, who will act as a driving force in his life and the story. Kopenkin is perhaps the most typically Quixotic, picaresque, and nomadic of all the characters. Like Sasha, he belongs nowhere, and he is driven by a desire that is also tied to death. He is a communist knight, and his point of orientation is his love for "Rosa," meaning Rosa Luxemburg. He regards Communism as a sensitive female who demands heroic deeds and tenderness, but it is highly telling that the object of his desire is not a living being but a dead person who needs a proper place for her grave. Lacking direction, Kopenkin and his horse wander about somewhat half-consciously. It is the horse, called "Revolutionary Force," that decides where to go, setting off as soon as it hears the name "Rosa." Kopenkin is certain that there is no reason for him to think or try to master his fate, because he knows "the common life to be wiser than his own head (obshchaia zhizn' umnei svoei golovy") (110).

Kopenkin is the first entirely "headless" enthusiast of the Revolution that we meet as a hero in the novel, and thus in a way he foreshadows or represents a kind of first sketch of the Chevengur inhabitants we will encounter further on. In fact, a central point about the characters is that they are firmly and utterly convinced that something must be done and someone is guilty, but they have no idea what and who, and many of them sense that they are not really at home in their own cognitive faculties. "Communist power," Dvanov thinks, is "the kingdom of a multitude of nondescript people of nature" ("Sovietskaia vlast' – eto tsarstvo mnozhestva prirodnykh nevzrachnykh liudei") (168), and Kopenkin himself asserts that he is a representative not of power but "a natural force" (Kakaia tebie vlast', my – prirodnaia sila!") (ibid.). This, however, is not something that must be thought—on the contrary, it appears as the necessary course of events. Kopenkin and Dvanov, therefore, support these people and join them in their struggle, although it seems to lack direction, accessible points of orientation, and political left or right.

As children of nature given for the first time a chance "to use their heads," the people of the Russian provinces are under the highly disorienting influence of revolutionary slogans. The Revolution is ecstatic and elemental, which leads to grotesque visions of the implementation of the rational logic of the new communist regime. When, for instance, Dvanov and Kopenkin arrive at the commune "The Poor Man's Friendship" ("Druzhba bedniaka"), they are enthusiastic until they discover that the new order of things has turned everyone there into a party functionary, with the result that no one has been able to plough the land and there is no bread. Kopenkin asks Sasha whether it wouldn't be best to liquidate the commune immediately, since it is impossible to decide who is the oppressor in this complicated life after the Revolution.

The characters of *Chevengur* are intensely and enthusiastically driven by the whims of a nearly absurd existence that seems to promise the utopia of Communism, but in the end offers no stable ground for understanding its realization. No one can "read" the world intelligently, and no one has a key to the hidden and uncanny idea of the Revolution. All are living an existence suffused with enthusiasm, and they attempt to fathom the upheaval as based on a new rationality. The problem is the dual promise of the Revolution: on the one hand, it is based on a rational and historical, dialectical, and political interpretation of existence according to which it would usher in the utopia of life as self-organizing happy and just activity. On the other hand, Platonov explores how the possibility of this utopian life as a headless self-organizing principle is duped by the very rationality of the revolutionary slogans. The depoliticization of life is caught up in the politics that were to bring it about. This is not a simple critique suggesting that things could be otherwise. It is a reflection on how being always appears as other to itself.

CHEVENGUR AND THE REALIZATION OF COMMUNISM

There is a second beginning in the novel—a second chance for the world and its revolutionaries. This is the start of the narrative about the city of Chevengur,[17] but it is a beginning that comes after the end. Chevengur, whose organizing committee declares that Communism has prevailed, is indeed a true dystopia. One of the crucial problems is that communist society presents itself as a new transcendental existence. It is a reality under constant and permanent emergency rule that understands itself as existing "after history." It is therefore a nonplace that arises after the end of the world and after history. It is the ultimate staging of the Revolution as transcendent and ideal rationality, but it becomes ultimate unreason running amok in the characters' attempts to form a consciousness, and all it offers are new forms of possession of man and nature.

The city of Chevengur is a truly ecstatic place situated on the borders of reason—on the boundary between man as a citizen and as an animal, between nature and civilization. The focus is once more on the way that the Revolution is supposed to offer a new reality to people "who are thinking for the first time" yet do not know how to implement it, and err by succumbing to the Bolshevik rationalization of history. Chepurnyi, who heads the struggle for Chevengur Communism, has never read Marx, nor, as he confesses, is he able to think himself (204):

> This was a misfortune for Chepurnyi and his rare comrades. Nowhere, neither in books nor in fairy tales, was communism written out as a comprehensible song that might be recalled for comfort in a dangerous hour. Karl Marx looked down from the walls like an alien Sabaoth, and his fearsome books could not carry a man off in reassuring daydreams about communism. Posters in Moscow and the provinces depicted a hydra of counterrevolution and trains filled with calico and broadcloth chugging into villages that had cooperatives, but nowhere was there a touching picture of that future, for the sake of which the hydra's head had to be lopped off and the heavy freight trains had to be pulled. Chepurnyi was forced to rely solely on his own inspired heart and its difficult strength in order to gain the future, whacking the souls out of the pacified bourgeoisie and embracing the walking blacksmith on the road. (199f.)

> [Но зато горе было Чепурному и его редким товарищам — ни в книгах, ни в сказках, нигде коммунизм не был записан понятной песней, которую можно было вспомнить для утешения в опасный час; Карл Маркс глядел со стен, как чуждый Саваоф, и его страшные книги не могли довести человека до успокаивающего воображения коммунизма; московские и губернские плакаты изображали гидру контрреволюции и поезда с ситцем и сукном, едущие в кооперативные деревни, но нигде не было той трогательной картины будущего, ради которого следует отрубить голову гидре и везти груженые поезда. Чепурный должен был опираться только на свое воодушевленное сердце и его трудной силой добывать будущее, вышибая души из затихших тел буржуев и обнимая пешехода-кузнеца на дороге.] (247)

Chepurnyi and his comrades would like to have Communism "written out as a comprehensible song that might be recalled for comfort," but instead "Karl Marx looked down from the walls like an alien Sabaoth." Thus, instead of a song that would humbly and intimately accompany them as a comforting memory, in the Bolsheviks' slogans and posters, Communism became a frightening Old Testament image of doomsday, and this is how its leader Chepurnyi comes to stage it. In the passage that contains the description of Chepurnyi's reflection on his ability to appropriate Communism, all the desperate moves that he takes are listed. He will attempt both literally and metaphorically "to knock the soul out of the silenced bodies of the bourgeoisie and embrace the blacksmith-wanderer on the road." Because Chepurnyi sees the bourgeoisie as an obstacle to Communism as the end of history, he has liquidated them so that even "their souls are penetrated by bullets" (225). Having read somewhere that the Soviet regime is ready to give the heavenly domains to the bourgeoisie while the earth will remain with the proletariat, he begins to liquidate them cruelly as the second coming of Christ that they were awaiting. The executions are grotesque, but no one seems to be appalled or sense any abnormality in the situation. This is how they understand the higher logic of the Revolution, and there is no other rationality to oppose to it, only a sense of alienation.

Both concretely and metaphorically, Chepurnyi and his comrades attempt to make this world their home. They go from one house to the next and even start to move houses and streets. After the liquidation of the bourgeoisie, deportation and migration begin. As they relocate these houses and trees, which are rooted in earth and in history, they discover that the city lacks manpower and women. At this point they start to reorganize the world to suit their needs. They decide to import the poor and "the miscellaneous" from the surrounding villages or just pick them up on the road, because the fact of Socialism in Chevengur needs the support of the masses to stabilize it:

> "And bring in the miscellaneous too. Socialism is a fact here."
> "Every fact without the support of the masses has its own instability, comrade Chepurny." (225)

> ["И прочего веди. Социализм у нас факт."
> "Всякий факт без поддержки масс имеет свою неустойчивость, товарищ Чепурный."] (260)

These "miscellaneous" people are residents of the orphanage that is the countryside; they are the provincial precariat with absolutely no name, history, or identity. They have been colonized by the communist society of Chevengur and made into just a new subjected class. It is of course no wonder that Chepurnyi fails. As it attempts to realize the transcendence of socialism, all the Revolution leads to is a new and absurd hegemonic production of social reality. Needless to say, the governance of the city and the reality itself depicted in *Chevengur* are out of control. There is no rationality to hold on to, because reason and unreason have fused in a grotesque machine for the realization of the Revolution through reorganizing the world, liquidating, transporting, and so forth. In the end, Chevengur will lose in the civil war and its inhabitants will all perish.

It is precisely in the parallel between the story of Dvanov's father's attempt to attain the transcendent realm of the fishes in Lake Mutevo and the realization of Communism that Platonov can address the problem of this realization. As he writes in a passage that well illustrates the logic and style of the strangeness of his language:

> Communism tormented Chepurnyi the way the secret of life after death had tormented Dvanov's father. Chepurnyi could not bear the mystery of time, so he cut short the length of history by the rapid

construction of communism in Chevengur, just as the fisherman Dvanov could not bear his own life and so had transformed it into death, in
order to experience the beauty of that world. (274)[18]

[Чепурного же, . . . коммунизм мучил, как мучила отца Дванова
тайна посмертной жизни, и Чепурный не вытерпел тайны
времени и прекратил долготу истории срочным устройством
коммунизма в Чевенгуре, — так же, как рыбак Дванов не вытерпел
своей жизни и превратил ее в смерть, чтобы заранее испытать
красоту того света.] (318)

Again we see how *Erlebte Rede* allows for a blend of first and third
person perspective that portrays something that seems to come from both
outside and inside an inconspicuous flow of the mind. It creates an in-
between inside and outside, where Platonov can depict characters without the ability to reflect on their own position and also without interfer-
ing with the author's comments. Further, the fusion of abstract and concrete levels contributes to the impression of a flow without reflection. For
instance, we are told that "Communism tormented" Chepurnyi, that is,
not that the idea, problems, or course of Communism tormented him, but
Communism itself. How? Communism tormented him "the way the secret of life after death had tormented Dvanov's father." In other words,
Communism tormented Dvanov as "the secret of life after death." It is
not enough to say that Communism acquires religious dimensions here,
because it really also becomes an existential question. Because of the way
that Communism torments Chepurnyi, he could not bear the "mystery of
time." In other words, he could not bear time, which is a mystery, the
mystery of the in-between life and death. Having established this existential aspect of Chepurnyi's relation to Communism, Platonov returns to a
language permeated by the bureacratism of communist language, once
more in an inconspicuous conflation of different perspectives, arguments
and registers of language, to establish that the leader of Chevengur "cut
short the length of history by the rapid construction of communism."
There seems to be a sarcastic suggestion of the historical eschatology of
dialectical materialism, but it is coated in the mind of the impatient Chepurnyi, who simply cannot bear that Communism as the secret of death
is not already at hand. Just like the fisherman, therefore, Chepurnyi en-
gages in a construction aimed at the impossible attainment of the secret
of death in life, or at experiencing "the beauty of that world." Finally, as
we learn in a most dismally unsentimental phrasing, he does so by transforming life into death. In other words, what Platonov depicts Chepurnyi
as doing in his realization or construction of Communism is not bringing
the secret of death to life, but on the contrary, turning life into death.

The dystopia of the novel consists in showing how the people—that is,
the Russian provincial population—attempt to establish a new transcendental home in the new communist postrevolutionary world as a home in

history. The absurdity and grotesqueries that this search leads to expose all the more clearly that in his grasp of the world, man is at home neither in himself nor in the world, and is rendered homeless particularly by the way in which history defines his understanding. Those who "think for the first time" are guided by the words of the Revolution, but this only results in disorientation and disaster. In fact, what the novel portrays is that subjectivity is a dystopia in which the people are not at home. Instead, one can say that in *Chevengur,* Platonov discovers and develops the problem of the realization of Communism.[19]

The idea of realization as a process of actualizing a potential, or as the famous horizon of Communism to come, is portrayed as one of the crucial reasons for this communist limbo fraught with destruction. Communism is always realized and yet to be realized.[20] Therefore, the characters wait and wait for this something, which at the same time had come, and Platonov draws our attention to how this state of limbo creates constant boredom and longing in his characters. They do not see the in-between of time or the way that people live on in each other but seek to assert themselves in projections of the future. Platonov invites us to think this problem in the historical schema of the revolution not solely in relation to Communism, as the problem of the communist utopia, but really as a profound problem of modernity in its "fear of finitude." Modernity, which is determined by the pattern of historical succession and the loss of metaphysics, thinks of continuity as the replacement of one time by another, and, if we follow Platonov, will therefore constantly chase its linear projection and be blind to the incongruities of the time.

The problem of the realization of utopia, in other words, is intimately related to the problem of time. Following the Marxist Hegelian scheme of the realization of consciousness, Soviet society projects itself as a transition and a transfer in terms of realizing the new. Jameson (1994) establishes a kinship between Platonov's understanding of utopia and Marx's insistence on a utopian imagination that realizes an unconscious dream in reality.[21] According to Marx, making the world conscious would mean the realization of this dream.[22] However, Platonov problematizes precisely this schema of consciousness. He stops us at the very moment of the in-between of the transfer between the old and the new, between utopia and its realization, between the unconscious and the conscious, the dream and awakening, and there he points at the impossibility of a transfer and a transition between these oppositions. It is not only that in *Chevengur* he points with Chepurnyi at the disastrous tragedy of the urge to "cut short the mystery of time" while insisting on the rapid construction of Communism—that is, on the rapid realization of its utopia. He also constantly depicts his characters in their attunement to the world as unable to form a conscious relation to it and to themselves. Communist consciousness in the form of the people's appropriations of party slogans is not a deeper awareness of being but an ecstatic and headless quest for the dream of

Communism. Time in *Chevengur* is "out of joint" and without a Hamlet to set it right. His heroes are either completely enmeshed in the ecstasy of a transcendent revolutionary time or they walk wearily about in search for a relation to time, and seem unable to find one, at least in a conscious condition.

Yet the force of Platonov's writing lies in precisely the fact that he does not look for a hero to resolve these incongruities, this out-of-joint time, in a transcendental position but portrays these unconscious dreams that cannot find a realization in society as the utopian truth about our times. He turns our attention to a literary revolutionary utopia of common being that is real to the extent that it is there in the form of the dream lost to Dvanov, where the world is present to him in all its undifferentiated difference.

NOTES

1. See the commentaries to the manuscripts in Platonov (2009, 539 f.).

2. Cf. Bethea (1989, 168), who writes, "To begin with, the novel is, compositionally, the opposite of a *Bildungsroman*: the temporal unfolding of Sasha's life is *not accompanied* by a growth in knowledge, a sense of domestic or societal 'fitting in,' a slow, but ultimately triumphant groping for the truth."

3. As Platonov remarks in "Otvet redaktsii": "Вы видите только наши заблуждения, а не можете понять, что не блуждаем мы, а ищем. Мы идем снизу, помогите нам, верхние, в этом мой ответ. для живого нет безобразия" (Platonov 2011b, 15). (You see only our errors and cannot understand that we are not erring but searching. We are coming from below. Help us, you above. That is my answer. There is no ugliness for the living.) See the discussion in the previous chapter.

4. In "Catastrophes in the Air," Joseph Brodsky (1986, 290) astutely describes this quality of Platonov's prose as follows: "Unlike Kafka, Joyce, and, let's say, Beckett, who narrate quite natural tragedies of their 'alter egos,' Platonov speaks of a nation which in a sense has become the victim of its own language; or, to put it more accurately, he tells a story about this very language, which turns out to be capable of generating a fictitious world, and then falls into grammatical dependence on it."

5. "What is the problem of the transcendental *locus* if not to determine how every impulse which springs from the innermost depths is co-ordinated with a form that is ignorant of, but that has been assigned to it from eternity and must envelop it in liberating symbols?" (Lukács 988, 29).

6. Lukács writes, "The novel form is, like no other, an expression of this transcendental homelessness" (Lukács 1971, 41). What Lukács means by "transcendental homelessness" can be understood from his description of the contrary state of being transcendentally at home. His foremost example of such a transcendental home is the world of Ancient Greece, a world that spoke to man in an understandable way, "when the sky is the map of all possible paths," as the *Theory* begins (1971, 29). Thus, transcendence can be understood as the possibility of a correspondence or even a coincidence between the spiritual or metaphysical and the concrete or physical lying beyond or perhaps surrounding the experiencing literary subject. The sky as a "roof" is not beyond but on the borders, and these borders speak to man about his possibilities in the world. According to Lukács, the experience of a transcendental home is possible only fragmentarily in lyrical poetry, where the lyrical I can give expression to an experience in which the world speaks, whereas in the modern novel there is no expression for man's being at home in the world.

7. Lukács (1971, 80) writes, "The inner form of the novel has been understood as the process of the problematic individual's journeying towards himself, the road from dull captivity within a merely present reality—a reality that is heterogeneous in itself and meaningless to the individual—towards clear self-recognition. After such self-recognition has been attained, the ideal thus formed irradiates the individual's life as its immanent meaning; but the conflict between what is and what should be has not been abolished and cannot be abolished in the sphere wherein these events take place—the life sphere of the novel; only a maximum conciliation—the profound and intensive irradiation of a man by his life's meaning—is attainable. The immanence of meaning which the form of the novel requires lies in the hero's finding out through experience that a mere glimpse of meaning is the highest that life has to offer, and that this glimpse is the only thing worth the commitment of an entire life, the only thing by which the struggle will have been justified. The process of finding out extends over a lifetime, and its direction and scope are given with its normative content, the way towards a man's recognition of himself."

8. Hans Günther (2011, 42) offers in passing a reading of *Chevengur* against the backdrop of Lukács's *Theory of the Novel*.

9. Cf. Hans Günther's (2011) comments on the importance of memory in the novel in the chapter "Mezhdu Pamiatiu i Utopiei."

10. All quotes from *Chevengur* in the Russian original are from the Vremia edition (Platonov 2009), indicated hereafter only by page number.

11. All translations of *Chevengur* are from Platonov and Anthony Olcott (1978), indicated below by page number only.

12. On this theme, see also Natalya Kornienko's article (2005), in which she compares *Chevengur* to his articles in the 1920s. Of particular interest is "Pitomnik novogo cheloveka," in which Platonov asserts that "Nature is much more immense, and complex than it appears when you are awake" ("Priroda bolee ogromna i bolee slozhna, chem naiavu.") (quoted in Kornienko 2005, 506.)

13. In the traditional realist novel, transgressive moments of illness, sleep or delirium are for the most part treated as distinct from the condition of the composed and conscious subject. In contrast, Platonov renders these moments equally or even more revealing of the hero's experience of existence. Unlike, for instance, Tolstoy's presentation of Prince Volkonsky's delirium in *War and Peace*, Dvanov's condition is not presented as an extraordinary state in which he experiences the world differently than he would if conscious.

14. Sic; "bodrstvuiushchii" would be better translated as "vigilant."

15. See Podoroga (1991, 36).

16. Indeed, if Platonov's striving for the abject and formless can be likened to Bataille's aesthetics, the main point of divergence is his search for an understanding of how beyond the laws of desire we encompass within ourselves the world, the all. Symptomatic of Bataille's approach is the title "The Object of Desire Is the Universe or the Totality of Being" (1997, 264).

17. The part about Zakhar Pavlovich initially belonged to another story "The Origins of the Master" ("Proiskhozhdenie mastera"), and the Chevengur part to "Builders of the Country" ("Stroiteli strany"); see Malygina (2009, 540).

18. Cf. the discussion of this passage in Jameson (1994, 117).

19. Cf. Seifrid (1996, 242), who proposes to label Platonov's masterpieces "ironic non-reification." Audun J. Mørch (1998, 186) also notes this problem. He conjectures a triangular equilibrium between utopia (nonplace), eutopia (happy place), and realization, and argues that this equilibrium must be maintained for utopia to be at work.

20. On the process of realization, or of making real socialism in postrevolutionary society, see Petrov (2011).

21. Indeed, this idea illustrates the correlation between the Marxist notion of alienation and Heidegger's forgetting of being: *Seinsvergessenheit*. Both concepts are guided by the idea that there is a lost relation to being that can be retrieved.

22. In a famous quote from a letter to his friend Arnold Ruge, Marx (2005, 144) wrote, "Then people will see that the world has long possessed the dream of a thing — and that it only needs to possess the consciousness of this thing in order to really possess it."

THREE

The Foundation Pit and the Problem of Time

Toward the end of the 1920s, Soviet society was undergoing a transition from a revolutionary phase to the period of the State Plans (*Gosplany*), and the large-scale project of building new houses (*Sovetskii stroi*). According to official propaganda, the Revolution had succeeded, and now the foundation was to be laid for the building of a new society. Platonov does not fail to thematize and register this change in his writings. To begin with, the style of *The Foundation Pit* differs from that of *Chevengur*, for instance, in that the principle of formlessness has given way to an allegorical conceptual structure. Arguably, the philosophical underpinnings remain; the conceptual style still serves to capture the paradox that existence in common constantly evades our conceptualizations of it. Further, the new era of construction and building is the theme of *The Foundation Pit*. The novel tells the allegorical story of the failed excavation of a foundation pit for the future house of the proletariat, and it ends with one of the workers of the team digging an abysmal grave for the orphaned girl Nastia, who in the mind of the diggers was to have crowned the future. Characteristically, Platonov shows that the work for the utopian promise of a happy social life embodied in the house of the proletariat is fraught with destruction, alienation, and death. The people have no other access to experience than their appropriation of official slogans that constantly refer them to the projection of utopia onto future institutionalizations. In direct negative proportion to propaganda for the building of the future house of the proletariat, Platonov portrays how people become duped by the propaganda and, unable to communicate with their experience, ultimately become preoccupied with death and liquidation rather than building.[1]

The novel is not only a grotesque and dark satire over Soviet society of the period; it also treats the question of time and historical succession with regard to the legacy of the Revolution, because the Revolution is established as a point zero that eliminates all other forms of legacies. By the late 1920s, the Revolution definitely becomes a moment of the past; it is declared completed and needing only to be materialized in the promise of future happiness. Behind the past Revolution there is another "bourgeois" past that has been irretrievably surpassed yet must still be liquidated. The novel takes place in the present and asks about the place of experience in an existence oriented toward the future realization of happiness. It serves to illustrate a problem of modern society in general, where time and place have emerged as the principal measure of life and the measures of finitude have become central points of orientation. Platonov depicts a society that is set on the future realization of communality and, therefore, continuously destroys the forms of experience of the common, thereby producing an increasing sense of groundlessness. Yet in this alienated and alienating rush toward the future, Platonov depicts people who are longing for an experience of existence in common, be it in the form of a memory of dream or of the warmth of a sleeping body close by. In the chiastic reversal that plays a formative role in the novel, the foundation of the house becomes destruction, and strangely enough, destruction becomes a home, assuring us that in its inner, the earth can harbor the victims of the historical scheme of progress.

THE LOSS OF TEMPO AND THE LOSS OF THE WORLD

The Foundation Pit is one of the more proletarian of Platonov's novels, in the sense that the central allegory of the book is related to work, to digging. Nevertheless, the novel begins with a farewell to the urban proletariat that identifies itself with organization and tempo. It opens as Voshchev loses both his job and his foothold in society.

> His dismissal notice stated that he was being removed from production on account of weakening strength in him and thoughtfulness amid the general tempo of labor. (1)[2]
>
> [В увольнительном документе ему написали, что он устраняется с производства вследствие роста слабосильности в нем и задумчивости среди общего темпа труда.] (Platonov 2009, 413)[3]

The beginning performs the double function of introducing both the plot and the theme of the book, which coincide on an allegorical level. We are immediately told that the main protagonist's social and working life does not admit of reflection, and that because he cannot refrain from thinking, Voshchev is expelled from the productive life of the proletariat. Thus, the notion of time and time measured as a means of exclusion is framed from the outset. In a way characteristic of Platonov, this exclusion does not result from or lead to any feeling of estrangement or hostility. Voshchev does not want to deviate—on the contrary, he wants to come up with "a plan of shared, general life," (3) thus echoing the "truth common to all and a meaning of life" of which Chepurnyi in his tragedy in *Chevengur* did not know. This "plan of shared, general life" is what would result in happiness; not according to the workplace administration, however, which dismisses Voshchev. According to the party representative, happiness originates not from thought but from materialism:

> Happiness will originate from materialism, comrade Voshchev, not from meaning. There's nothing we can do on your behalf. You are a man without consciousness and we don't want to find ourselves at the tail end of the masses. (4)

> [Счастье произойдет от материализма, товарищ Вощев, а не от смысла. Мы тебя отстоять не можем, ты человек несознательный, а мы не желаем очутиться в хвосте масс.] (415)

The Russian expression for "there is nothing we can do on your behalf" ("My tebia otstoiat' ne mozhem"), contains the word *otstoiat'*, which means to defend someone. Because of Voshchev's pensiveness, there is no solidarity with him. The expression "at the tail end of the masses" ("v khvoste mass") is taken from official propaganda and served to spur enthusiasm and competition to maintain the tempo dictated by the state plans. At the same time that Platonov mocks this idea, he is also concerned about a deeper problem, namely the fear of finitude in a postmetaphysical society. This apprehension is not the dread of death but the fear of failure to keep pace, of lagging behind or ending up last. This anxiety leads to a new form of alienation for the worker. State organization will henceforth in the novel be juxtaposed to Voshchev's quest for a shared meaning of life, and the former seems to exclude the latter in the modern world.

When Voshchev loses his job, he also loses his social life, his knowledge of truth, and his energy:

> He walked on down the road until exhaustion; Voshchev got exhausted quickly, as soon as his soul remembered that it had stopped knowing truth. (5)

> [Он шел по дороге до изнеможения; изнемогал же Вощев скоро, как только его душа вспоминала, что истину она перестала знать.] (416)

In other words, he loses his world and his sense of meaning. The last outpost of his former life is a "beer room," where he has left part of himself and something that was "in common with his life" the night before:

Once again he had to go past the beer room on the outskirts of town; once again he looked at where he had spent the night—something in common with his own life still remained there—and then Voshchev found himself in space, with only the horizon before him and the feel of the wind against his downbent face. (4)

[Ему еще раз пришлось миновать пригородную пивную, еще раз он посмотрел на место своего ночлега—там осталось что-то общее с его жизнью, и Вощев очутился в пространстве, где был перед ним лишь горизонт и ощущение ветра в склонившееся лицо.] (416)

Voshchev is now utterly alone. Although he shares a great deal with the typical modern marginalized hero who shuns society, he keeps asking for and desiring this communality. The beginning of the novel presents the modern schema of alienation: the protagonist loses his initial state of naiveté and harmony, leaves his ordinary social reality, and reenters the world alienated and searching for "truth" and orientation. For him, the world now holds only meaninglessness, alienation and oblivion, and his voyage mostly resembles a lonely and exhausted stumbling about. Voshchev becomes an onlooker, "like someone living in absence" (9) ("zaochno zhivushchii") (419), and yet he keeps seeking to experience the world from within. Because his hopeless ruminations wear him out, he wishes to take part in the energy of work, engagement, and communality. He wants to discover a meaning of life that is common to all and will last a long time ("vesobshchii, dolgii smysl zhizni"). It is in the midst of this quest that Voshchev comes upon the construction site. At first, however, he sees only the "timber delirium of the scaffolding" (9) ("v tesovom bredu lesov") (420), and he declares that "man puts up a building and falls apart himself" (9). In the end he asks, "Who'll be left to live then?" a question that can be paraphrased as central to the novel: for whom will there be place in a world that is obsessed only with its own future construction?

MATTER AND ENERGY

What aligns Platonov with the existential thought of Martin Heidegger is that he does not describe the world apart from man's relation to it and does not separate man from his being in the world.[4] For Heidegger, the world is not an object; it always already implies the way that man is in the world.[5] He defines existence, *Dasein*, as *In-der-Welt-Sein*—that is, as being in the world. Platonov, of course, never uses Heidegger's terminology in his literary or essayistic works; indeed, it is unlikely that he was familiar in any depth with the phenomenological tradition. Common to both, nevertheless, is an understanding of man and the world not as two entities but as a relation of being in the world. The focus on this relationship and the desire to bring it out in the narrative is what motivates

Platonov's constant breaks with linguistic collocation and valency.[6] It is not that words are taken out of their "normal" context, but that Platonov shows that what his characters do, and encounter has a double meaning that is both concrete and existential and, is at the same time, active in our relation to the world. These dual meanings cannot be separated from each other, precisely because he portrays the world as a relation, a way of being *in* rather than an object. Therefore, these meanings intermingle in his heroes' approach to reality. This is most notable in the extreme case of a dying peasant who is barely breathing. One of the diggers asks him,

> "You breathing?"
> "When I remember, I sigh" weakly replied the man.
> "What if you forget to breathe?"
> "Then, I'll die."
> "Maybe you don't sense the meaning of life," said Voshchev to the supine man. "Just wait a little, be patient." (89f)

[Ты что — дышишь?
 Как вспомню, так вздохну, — слабо ответил человек.
 — А если забудешь дышать?
 — Тогда помру.
 — Может, ты смысла жизни не чувствуешь, так потерпи чуть-чуть, — сказал Вощев лежачему.] (486)

This focus on man's being in the world is what gives the allegory of *The Foundation Pit* its specific features. An allegorical reading of the excavation as a parable about Soviet society is made possible by the fact that this level is already present in the speech of the characters. They seek an existential meaning in their work and materials that often coincides with but also deviates from official propaganda. Because the project fails, the meaning of the official propaganda fails along with it. In other words, since the excavation of the foundation pit does not lead to the erection of the future house of the proletariat, the characters come to doubt the very meaning of future construction.

We also see Platonov's insistence on man as a being-in-the-world reflected in the existential qualities acquired by the landscape as Voshchev turns to the material or organic world that surrounds him in his quest for a "new" truth as a form of meaning. However, the natural world is not raw, pure, or innocent in any sense; while nature is always already a part of man's conception of it, in the modern world it has already become the product of a utilitarian, estranged society.[7] When Voshchev asks the air about his future, he finds it empty, and he surrounds himself with concrete "objects of unhappiness and obscurity" (5) ("predmety neschastiia i bezvestnosti,") (416). This is why Voshchev first approaches the pit as a place of both physical and existential rest. At first sight, all it seems to offer him is a place where he can sink or "lower himself" into the earth:[8]

Voshchev wandered into some empty wilderness and discovered a warm pit for the night; having lowered himself into this earthy hollow, he laid under his head the bag where he collected every kind of obscurity for memory and vengeance, felt sad and so fell asleep. (9)

[Вощев забрел в пустырь и обнаружил теплую яму для ночлега; снизившись в эту земную впадину, он положил под голову мешок, куда собирал для памяти и отмщения всякую безвестность, опечалился и с тем уснул.] (420)

The "empty wilderness" ("pustyr") is also a "superfluous place" ("lishnee mesto") that can temporarily host the restless hero in his moment of repose. Voshchev himself epitomizes the superfluous man ("lishnii chelovek") of Russian realist literature, a character whose predisposition for rumination renders him alienated, marginalized, or otherwise unable to take part in society. As for Voshchev, his superfluity derives from his inability to keep pace with the accelerated tempo of labor, and he dedicates his attention to extraneous things and places. The place for which he is destined, however, turns out to be the foundation pit—"kotlovan"—that will soon be "hidden forever beneath construction" (10) ["ono skoro skroetsia naveki pod ustroistvom"] (420). Here as well there is a suggestion of a double meaning with fatal implications. Particularly the emphatic word "naveki" (forever) combined with "kroetsia" (will be hidden) implies that the construction has consequences beyond the simple fact that the pit will no longer be there. Indeed, what is suggested is that superfluous places will forever be hidden.

Once more, Voshchev is expelled, as a superfluous man, from the pit to the barracks. He discovers the team of workers on the construction site and joins them. It is significant that he enters their community for the first time as they are sleeping. They are merely bodies—actually, just matter as different form of energy—and he lowers himself to sleep in their company. Sleep offers a peculiar form of communality and being in the world. It is opposed to the conscious world as a world where there seems to be a possible inward convergence of truth and experience. In the conscious world, both communality and individuality are given in ecstatic forms, because, as Heidegger writes in *Being and Time*, existence in time is being in the ex-, outside of the self. In *The Foundation Pit*, either people heedlessly congregate, or the lack of meaning and reflection wears them down and alienates them from each other. The experience of others through sleep, like the experience of sleep as such, however, is an experience of the common on the borders of articulate experience. Sleep thus tells the characters about the existence of another life or form of life or being in the world that is different from what they can represent to themselves in their different ecstatic states of consciousness.

Voshchev, who cannot help looking for meaning in whatever he does, turns as he works to the earth in the pit for an answer about the truth of existence. He digs "as though wanting to obtain truth from amid the earth's dust" ("tochno khotel dobyt' istinu iz zemnogo prakha"):

> The mowed wilderness smelled of grass that had died and the dampness of bared places, making more palpable the general sorrow of life and the vain melancholy of meaninglessness. Voshchev was given a spade, and he gripped it in his hands with the ferocity of despair of his own life, as though wanting to obtain truth from amid the earth's dust: dispossessed as he was, Voshchev was even willing to do without the meaning of existence, but he wished at least to observe it in the substance of the body of another, neighboring man—and to find himself near such a man he was ready to sacrifice in labor the whole of his own weak body that had been exhausted by thought and senselessness. (12)

> [На выкошенном пустыре пахло умершей травой и сыростью обнаженных мест, отчего яснее чувствовалась общая грусть жизни и тоска тщетности. Вощеву дали лопату, он сжал ее руками, точно хотел добыть истину из земного праха; обездоленный, Вощев согласен был и не иметь смысла существования, но желал хотя бы наблюдать его в веществе тела другого, ближнего человека, — и чтобы находиться вблизи того человека, мог пожертвовать на труд все свое слабое тело, истомленное мыслью и бессмысленностью.] (422)

"Exhausted by thought and senselessness," Voshchev seeks to retrieve energy and meaning both from the earth that he digs and from his proletarian companions, in the "substance of the body of another, neighboring man." Again there is a sinking movement as Voshchev lowers himself, probing a world he finds organic and barren. What he finds, however, is not any truth or sheer force, but bodies and people who are as trapped as he is in a world that produces and uses "dead matter." Hence, Voshchev, once again, begins to doubt whether he will really find any meaning in his work:

> Voshchev returned to digging the unchanging clay and he saw that there still remained a lot of clay and general earth—he would need to possess life for a long time in order to overcome, by means of oblivion and labor, this embedded world that had hidden in its own darkness the truth of all existence. Maybe it would be easier to think up the meaning of life in his head—after all, he might hit on it inadvertently or touch it with some sadly flowing feeling. (195–96)

> I'd be better off thinking without working [my translation; T. L.].

> [Вощев . . . видел, что глины и общей земли еще много . . . — еще долго надо иметь жизнь, чтобы превозмочь . . . трудом этот залегший мир, спрятавший в своей темноте истину всего существования. Может быть, легче выдумать смысл жизни в голове — ведь можно нечаянно догадаться о нем или коснуться его печально текущим чувством . . . лучше я буду думать без работы, все равно весь свет не разроешь до дна.] (424; ellipses in original)

In this passage, which was reconstructed from the publisher's manuscript of the novel,[9] Platonov repeats and reinforces some of the thoughts
in the previously quoted passage. In an intriguing play on words that
mixes metaphorical and concrete senses, he conveys how man's being in
the world determines his understanding of reality and meaning. Applied
to the earth, the metaphor of "hidden truth" suggests that truth really is
concealed in the earth beneath all the inert matter. Voshchev "sees" different layers of a world that is embedded ("zalegshii") below, and under
them he senses the presence of the "truth of all existence" ("istinu svoego
sushchestvovaniia"). The quotation, however, has an even more conspic-
uous pun on the metaphor "kopat'sia ili dokopat'sia," which literally
translates as "to dig down to meaning," and metaphorically means "to
reach the truth." In the first sentence, it is as if Voshchev is indeed searching for a correspondence between metaphorical and concrete meaning,
without, however, subordinating one to the other.[10] He really wants to
dig up the truth by means of physical labor. He cannot excavate "the
truth of all existence" because the earth has too much clay in it, and he
must, therefore, "overcome it by labor" ("prevozmoch' . . . trudom").
Here the metaphorical and concrete meanings coincide: the clay is dead
matter lying in wait in a dead world.[11]

Understanding the world as inert matter is what concretely renders it
inert or dead. Consequently, we come to see not only the world but also
nature as dead. Thus, Platonov shows how concrete meanings corre-
spond to the metaphors through which people understand the world,
and conversely, how metaphorical meaning in the concrete world that
they encounter is waiting to be dug up. In this world there are no stable
relations between the metaphorical and the concrete; moreover, there is
no purely concrete meaning which has not been taken up in the "organized" world and its metaphorical language. Thus, Platonov digs into
language and undermines it, showing that it is already enmeshed in existence and that we must understand the relationship between metaphor
(transposed meaning) and concrete meaning as a correspondence that is
always already at work in the world and can never be undone.

Epitomizing the consequence of a materialist a priori understanding
of reality, Prushevskii, who represents the Marxist intellectual and engineering mind, sees the whole world as dead matter ("мертвый
материал," 422) or as a "dead body" (12). Parallel to Voshchev, he reflects as follows on the soil:

> Prushevsky was chilled from the night and he climbed into the pit that
> had been begun for the foundations. It was quiet there, and for some
> time he sat in its depth. There was rock beneath him, and the walls of
> the excavation rose up on either side of him; he could see how the
> topsoil rested on a layer of clay and did not originate from it. Could a
> superstructure develop from any base? Was soul within man an inevi-
> table by-product of the manufacture of vital material? And if produc-

tion could be improved to the point of precise economy, would it give rise to other oblique by-products? (19–20)

[Прушевский остыл от ночи и спустился в начатую яму котлована, где было затишье. Некоторое время он посидел в глубине; под ним находился камень, сбоку возвышалось сечение грунта, и видно было, как на урезе глины, не происходя из нее, лежала почва. Изо всякой ли базы образуется надстройка? Каждое ли производство жизненного материала дает добавочным продуктом душу в человека? А если производство улучшить до точной экономии — то будут ли происходить из него косвенные, нежданные продукты?] (428–29)

The word "zatishie" ("hush" or "quiet") in the Russian original lends the description a fairy-tale quality and creates an idyllic rural atmosphere. It places us in a landscape viewed from the "depth" of the pit and invites the reader to reflect on the soil in existential terms. Prushevskii looks into this "depth" and sees the "topsoil" ("pochva") and immediately asks himself the classic Marxist questions: Could a superstructure develop from any base? Was soul within man an inevitable by-product of the manufacture of vital material? Here, however, the Marxist metaphor acquires not only concrete meaning but also a new metaphorical sense, gaining metaphysical ground as it extends to the soul and all existence. Thus, when Prushevskii asks the very telling question whether any "living material" ("zhiznennogo materiala," or, in the translation above, "vital material") can be generated in the soul as a byproduct, he at the same time inquires whether a happy, soulful house can result from this pit and its soil. The question is where happiness will come from. Or, as Prushevskii frames it, where does that "extra/ superfluous warmth that once was called the soul" originate? In Platonov's world, nothing comes from nothing; the living world must come from the living, and, happiness is unlikely to emerge from unhappiness. Or, as the expression "Chto v kotel polozhish, to i vynesh" has it, all that comes out of the kettle/cauldron is what you put into it. As Platonov suggests, therefore, treating the earth as inert matter will also make the earth inert matter. Thus, he deconstructs Bolshevik materialism to mean "dead material" and shows how the physical world, in terms of both man and objects, is subjected to this conception. In those terms, Bolshevik materialism implies a denial of the way in which the world as a phenomenon speaks to us, but the way that the world speaks to is to us is precisely what Voshchev (and Platonov) seeks to retrieve.

KOTLOVAN AND COMMUNALITY

Because Platonov's depiction of reality is based on man's being in the world, the meaning of the pit and the idea behind *Kotlovan* will be more than the earth that is being excavated. Moreover, the pit will prove to be more than earth or clay. History, materialized in the coffins that the workers find, lives on in the earth. Indeed, the word "kotlovan" itself derives from "kotel," which means pothole, cauldron, or kettle and also connotes a hotchpotch, a miscellaneous collection of things. Platonov plays on this meaning of the word, as for instance in the conversation between Voshchev and a kolkhoz "activist":

> "And truth?" asked Voshchev. "Is truth the due of the proletariat?"
>
> "Movement is the due of the proletariat," summarized the activist, "along with whatever the proletariat comes across on the way. Doesn't matter if it's truth or a looted kulak jacket—it'll all go into the organized cauldron till you won't be able to recognize anything at all." (78f)

> [А истина полагается пролетариату? спросил Вощев. Пролетариату полагается движение, произнес активист, а что навстречу попадается, то все его: будь там истина, будь кулацкая награбленная кофта — все пойдут в организованный котел, ты ничего не узнаешь.] (477)

According to the activist, the world of the proletariat is an "organized" pothole that is driven not by the truth, but by movement. Here anything can appear, and it is difficult to make out what is what. The "kotel" or cauldron is a metaphor for the life and new culture of the proletariat, which must not ask about what kind of existence they find along the way—be it truth or a "looted kulak jacket"—but merely keep in step with the tempo and forms of organization. The juxtaposition of truth and stolen clothing is another typical example of the way that Platonov fuses concrete and abstract, literal, and metaphorical. This "stolen jacket" must be read not as a metaphor of the kind of existence that the proletariat will find, but as the concrete object. What the activist tells us is that what the proletariat encounters might just as well be truth as a jacket, thus making them equal on the ontological level.

Tempo also defines the motley worker brigade's understanding of their labor. None of the members of the group really have any place or sense of home in society. Besides Voshchev, we meet Chiklin, strong and physically attractive, who wanted to "cover" too many (women), and therefore, when everyone deserted him, started to act depraved and ended up in jail; Kozlov, a weak and sickly worker who lives only in hopes for the future; Prushevskii, the engineer, who enjoys the cold and clear indifference of his technical work and is left with only the childhood memory of an evening when a girl walked by his window and became "his only friend"; Zhachev, the cripple; Safronov, the brigade leader, who constantly echoes official propaganda; and Nastia, a young orphaned girl who is literally torn from her mother's body. Like the people of the kolkhoz in *Chevengur*, these workers will also think and attempt "for the first time" to appropriate revolutionary language and practice, but as in the earlier novel, their efforts will not lead to the establishment of a new home in the world. Platonov shows us that for the most part, the characters live ecstatically as they try to keep up with progress. Most workers hope that once the house is built, happiness will appear. Kozlov, for instance, "still believed in the life to come after the construction of the big buildings" (15) ("eshche veril v nastuplenie zhizni posle postroiki bol'shikh domov") (425). When new workers arrive, they will all "think up an idea of their future salvation" (43), or rather of "future happiness" ("kazhdyi iz nikh pridumal sebe ideiu budushchego shchastiia" (448). Thus, in a way that mirrors the future utopia of socialist construction, in their relationship with the building of the house, time is the measure or pace that determines the meaning of the work.

It is precisely the understanding of time as the tempo of labor and the promise of future happiness that hinders an understanding of truth, at least in the sense of comprehending existence. Questions of grounds, origins, and the afterlife of the bourgeois past are constantly brought to the fore. According to the Marxist historical schema of successive periods based on Hegel, a fundamental break is possible between different periods. However, the negation and destruction of the past seems to lead only to a deeper groundlessness. The activist calls for "an understanding of the meaning of 'de-membering'" (80). The afterlife of the past becomes particularly telling in the figure of Nastia, whose bourgeois mother has taught her to deny her past and proclaim herself a part of the communist future. And as Chiklin comments, Soviet power has anchored itself deeply if an unborn child remembers Communism but does not recall her own mother. It is also Nastia who most ardently insists on liquidating anything reminiscent of "bourgeois" behavior, because to her mind, everything that belongs to the past is bad and must be exterminated, and everything good will come in the future. This contrast is illustrated, for instance, in the conflict over the coffins that constitutes another very important story about the presence of the past and in the discussion about the problems of founding the future house of the proletariat. As they dig the foundation pit, the workers come upon a hundred coffins belonging to a nearby kolkhoz. They decide to keep at least two of them for Nastia to play and sleep in. In other words, rather than a jacket, they steal some coffins. Opposed to each other in this story are Nastia as the embodiment of the eternal future and the coffins, which testify to the presence of the past. An argument breaks out, and Nastia insists that the workers go and kill the owners of the coffins:

> "Go and kill them then!" said the little girl.
> "That's not allowed, my daughter. Two persons don't make a class."
> "There was one, and then another one," counted the little girl.
> "But overall there were still too few of them" regretted Safronov.
> "Our task, according to the plenum, is to liquidate them as a class and

nothing less—the landless laborers and the entire proletariat must be orphaned from their enemies!"

"Who will you be left with then"

"We'll be left with the tasks. With the hard line of the furthest measures—get what I mean?" (64)

["Убей их пойди!" сказала девочка.

"Не разрешается, дочка: две личности это не класс . . ."

"Это один да еще один," сочла девочка.

"А в целости их было мало," пожалел Сафронов. "Мы же, согласно пленума, обязаны их ликвидировать не меньше как класс, чтобы весь пролетариат и батрачье сословие осиротели от врагов!"

"А с кем останетесь?"

"С задачами, с твердой линией дальнейших мероприятий, понимаешь что?"] (465)

Nastia's understanding of history appears as a simple and satirical allusion to the historical schema of *diamat*, according to which one class will be liquidated and replaced by another. However, this not only leaves the people as orphans in the world, but also orphans time itself. The Revolution was preoccupied with destroying the old foundation of society to clear the way for a new culture and home in the world. Yet again, however, the question is whether in the existential or cultural respect this new home can become a true home if the world merely hides the previous reality in the alleged destruction of it in order for this new happy building to appear. As an inverted mirror of Nastia's reflection and foreshadowing the abysmal end, Prushevskii thinks that it is good if the workers die during their work with the foundation, because then they can all die together, leaving the past behind and open to receive the bright future.[12]

After the conversation between Nastia and Safronov, Voshchev distances himself, "content that he was no longer a participant in these insane circumstances" (65) ("uchastnik bezumnykh obstoiatel'stv") (466). He discovers the traces of the two coffins that the men have taken back, and he begins to think about what they mean and about time:

He looked around: everywhere the stream of living breath hung over space, creating a sleepy, stifling invisibility; endurance dragged on wearily in the world, as if everything living found itself somewhere in the middle of time and its own movement; its beginning had been forgotten by everyone; its end was unknown, and nothing remained but a direction to all sides. And so Voshchev disappeared down the only open road. (66)

[Он осмотрелся вокруг — всюду над пространством стоял пар живого дыханья, создавая сонную, душную незримость; устало длилось терпенье на свете, точно все живущее находилось где-то посредине времени и своего движения: начало его всеми забыто и

конец неизвестен, осталось лишь направление. И Вощев ушел в
одну открытую дорогу.] (466f.)

In contrast to the others, Voshchev observes time in nature. Nature
measures and understands time differently. Here it is in the middle, situated in between a forgotten past and an end that it cannot know. This in-
between is the time of Voshchev's existential landscape. Due to the historical schema according to which periods succeed each other, however,
there seems to be no place for it in life. The only thing to do is to embark
upon the road that will take him to the kolkhoz and the abysmal story of
the conflict between the owners of the coffins (the *podkulachniki*) and the
workers.

THE ABYSS

Because life has been transformed into dead material, death will be explored as a locus of life. At least as a negative parallel to the promise of
future happiness, the pit becomes the locus both of the workers' despair
and their hopes attached to death. Long before the failure of the project
becomes apparent to them, however, Prushevskii reflects on the ravine's
potential to become an abyss:

> They stopped at the edge of the gully foundation pit; they should have
> got down long ago to digging such an abyss for a communal home—
> then the being that Prushevsky needed would have stayed intact and
> complete there. (40)

> [Они остановились на краю овражного котлована; надо бы гораздо
> раньше начать рыть такую пропасть под общий дом, тогда бы и то
> существо, которое понадобилось Прушевскому, пребывало здесь в
> целости.] (445)

The remark is paradoxical and uncanny in an absurd way. When Prushevskii, qua architect, reflects on the material of the ravine, what he
considers is not its potential to serve as a foundation for the collective
house, but its ability to preserve the "being that Prushevsky needed"
("sushchestvo, kotoroe ponadobilos' Prushevskomu"). The being he
needs is Nastia's dead mother. She is to be kept in the abyss that they will
dig under the house. Platonov transforms the expression "dig such an
abyss" ("ryt' takuju propast'," based on the idiomatic expression "vyryt'
propast,'" meaning to dig an immense hole), into a multifaceted oxymoron: an abyss cannot be excavated, nor can it be a foundation for a house
or preserve anything. (On this last point, the connotations of the Russian
word "propast'" are even stronger than the English translation "abyss,"
for a "propast'" is where something "falls through" or "disappears"
("propadaet"). Instead of affirming that they should have started digging
such an abyss long ago, Prushevskii's oxymoron opens up a different

perspective on the chasm as a paradoxical place of disappearance where lost, dead, beloved beings can be kept in their nonbeing. Platonov also plays on the metaphorical meaning of the word "podryvat'" ("to undermine") in the expression "ryt' takuiu propast' pod obshchii dom," which in Russian literally means "to dig an abyss under the communal house." This house will be undermined by the abyss, in the sense that a society built on a construction of the future cannot entirely undo the afterlife of the past. The abyss will prove to be the home of the despair of the people, who cannot access their experience of the present.

It is in this ravine that Chiklin finds the empty coffins, which, as mentioned earlier, are another image of the presence of the past. In the end, the ravine becomes a grave. Chiklin and the men from the kolkhoz dig an abyss to bury Nastia:

> Chiklin took a crowbar and a new spade and walked slowly to the far border of the foundation pit. There he again began to gape the motionless earth wide open, since he was able to cry, and he went on digging, lacking the strength to exhaust himself, until nightfall, and all through the night, until he heard the cracking of bones in his labouring torso. Then he stopped and glanced around. The collective farm was following him and, without stopping, was digging the earth; all the poor and middle peasants were working with such zeal of life as if they were seeking to save themselves forever in the abyss of the foundation pit. (148)

> [Чиклин взял лом и новую лопату и медленно ушел на дальний край котлована. Там он снова начал разверзать неподвижную землю, потому что плакать не мог, и рыл, не в силах устать, до ночи и всю ночь, пока не услышал, как трескаются кости в его трудящемся туловище. Тогда он остановился и глянул кругом. Колхоз шел вслед за ним и не переставая рыл землю; все бедные и средние мужики работали с таким усердием жизни, будто хотели спастись навеки в пропасти котлована.] (533–34)

After Nastia's death, Chiklin digs out of grief, and the poor men join him, as if they wished to be saved forever "in the abyss of the foundation pit" ("v propasti kotlovana"). The abyss is where Chiklin can empty out his sorrow (he is now at one with his work), where the poor and nameless people from the kolkhoz can find shelter en masse, and in the end, where Nastia's grave can be placed and preserved. The tragic ending of the novel as the digging of an abyss is at the same time an opening into the earth and into a beyond that is both death and life, entrance and exit, being and nonbeing.

The world that confronts Voshchev and his fellow diggers is a world where a society that is preoccupied with man's realization of his happiness leads paradoxically only to unhappiness. Through an "inconspicuous paradoxicality" and an inconspicuous fusion of concrete and abstract meanings, Platonov shows how the characters seek to make sense of their existence but are unable to do so. The past is declared inimical and is targeted for liquidation; the present is an ousted and superfluous in-between, and the future; which is the locus onto which they project their happiness, becomes the promise of a happy congregation in death. Several scholars have read the promise of death in terms of a Fedorovian utopia according to which the salvation of the earth is connected with the resurrection of the dead. Whether or not Fedorov's philosophy was a source of inspiration, Platonov's focus is on the existential conditions that cause man to attach his hopes for future happiness to death. He shows men who are unable to retrieve a relation to life and therefore cannot make sense of their being-in-the-world. Death thus comes to appear as a more promising home for the experience of common being that cannot be contained in the people's projection of their understanding of life onto the future realization of happiness.

NOTES

1. This allegory has been read as an inverted utopia which embraces the thought of Nikolay Fedorov by insisting that we must make a place in the world for the dead, but I will argue that Platonov seeks a deeper existential meaning behind this philosophy.

2. All quotations are from Platonov and Chandler, et. al. (2009). References below will be by page number only.

3. References below to this edition will be by page number only.

4. Heidegger defines existence not as an entity, but as a relation: "Dasein is a being that does not simply occur among other beings. Rather it is ontically distinguished by the fact that in its being this being is concerned *about* its very being. Thus, it is constitutive of the being of Da-sein to have, in its very being, a relation of being to this being" (Heidegger 1996, 10).]

5. Heidegger defines "world" as a feature of existence: "'World' is ontologically not a determination of *those* beings which Dasein essentially is *not*, but rather a characteristic of Dasein itself" (1996, 60).

6. For a comprehensive linguistic account of Platonov's language, see Dhooge, 2007.

7. Magun (2010) describes Platonov's work as a kind of antimatter: "И действительно, сам Платонов сознает, что его произведения, как котлован, являются своеобразной антиматерией, питаются отрицательной энергией уничтожения, энергией отложенного умирания, усталости, смерти: 'Все, что я пишу, питается из какого-то разлагающегося вещества моей души.'" [And indeed, Platonov is himself aware that his works such as *The Foundation Pit* are a kind of antimatter, which are nourished by the negative energy of destruction, the energy of postponed dying, weariness, death: "Everything I write is nourished by some sort of decaying matter of my soul."]

8. Cf. Heidegger's notion of *Versunkenheit* in being.

9. See Malygina (2009, 583).

10. Platonov's puns on the concrete or literal and the metaphorical have been analyzed by several scholars. See, for instance, Apelboin (2002, 179) and Seifrid (1992, 199) terms this wordplay "awkward literalizations," Meerson (2001) refers to it as "re-familiarization" or a way of "normalizing" the abnormal or absurd. As she shows, in blurring the relationship between the normal and abnormal Platonov leaves undecided what the "literal," "normal," "re-familiarized" or "nonreified" meaning would

be. The relationship between the concrete and the metaphorical is unstable, while Platonov indicates that we cannot understand the concrete in an isolated way that is not already permeated by ontology.

11. Both in his novels and in his journalistic writing, Platonov frequently discusses the nature of the earth, soil, clay, and sand. Particularly interesting is "Pervyi Ivan (Zametki o tekhnicheskom tvorchestve trudiashchikhsia liudei)" (1930), where he links the condition of the earth to the economic system.

12. Kozlov's comment is also significant: "где раньше стол был явств, теперь там гроб стоит" ("Once the table groaned with fare, / Now there's just a coffin there") (66).

FOUR

Happy Moscow and Universal Love

With regard to length and intent, *Happy Moscow* (*Schastlivaia Moskva*) (Incomplete 1932–1936) is also among Platonov's major works. It was the second "novel" ("roman") that he attempted to write, but it remained unfinished, and its publications and translations are based on the unpublished manuscript. The fact that it was conceived as a novel testifies to the magnitude of the endeavor, and its title also suggests a certain grandeur of theme, since Moscow (Moskva), the name of the female protagonist, also alludes to the capital.[1] *Happy Moscow* is a conceptual tale about one of the main revolutionary promises of modern life in the crown jewel of the growing Soviet Empire: the promise of happiness under Communism. As Irina Sandomirskaja has pointed out, the word for happiness in Russian, *schast'e*, is related to the word for part (*chast'*), and usually refers to the notion of luck, in the sense of a good share or lot in life.[2] Furthermore, the word *schast'e* is also related to sharing and partaking, which is significant for our understanding of the novel, because the happiness that is at stake there is universal love. Moscow Chestnova embodies the Revolutionary fire as a force that aspires to work constantly to realize this love as the light for all that was one of Lenin's revolutionary promises. However, her imagination of love as light and happiness seems to force her not only to constantly rush forward, making her love for everyone merely cumulative in the sense of loving one person after the other; her path must also constantly be "uplit" and moving, in the sense that she literally wants light and movement around her constantly. This leads her to her tragic fate, her tragic lot, and thus Platonov asks whether the idea of happiness under Communism might not be another idea of universal love built on an idea of sharing that differs from the notion of universal love based on constant light and satisfaction of desire. Again for another vision of happiness and love he turns his attention to realms of the negative, the obscure and indifferentiated such as darkness and the night.

In accordance with Moscow Chestnova's dream of a constantly happy, moving, and "uplit" world, the modernizing project on which *Happy Moscow* and its language centers is electrification. The novel thematizes revolutionary electrification as a promise of future happiness that would not only spread real light and warmth in homes and cities but would also illuminate and warm the hearts and bodies of the people. In keeping with the theme of electrification, the central terminology around which the language and the narrative evolve has to do with energy.[3] Energy, which today means power, draws on the Greek word *energeia*—activity, to be at work. The two meanings coincide interestingly in the theme of the novel to denote a force or power at work in the production of future activity. Moscow Chestnova embraces the modernized Muscovite world in which she lives in an ecstatic, headless way and imagines the fire in her body as an enthusiastic flame that will fill the world with energy, light and warmth. She surges incessantly up and toward the future. Her elements are the sun and the wind, and it is telling that as a young girl she imagines herself or her body "carried upward [*vozneseno*] to a great height" (Platonov and Chandler, et al. 2012, 9).[4] The powerful drive for happiness makes her irresistibly attractive to men, whom she sets immediately on fire. It is as if her body carries the utopian energy that is also at work in different fields in the construction of Moscow at the time. This energy parallels the revolutionary promise to electrify the entire country and the development of the energy discourse in Soviet society. Just like the lights that constantly illuminate the capital, Moscow wants to spread her radiance to the world day and night. As usual, however, Platonov turns the concepts inside out, showing how the increase of light and Moscow Chestnova's love leads only to restless and fugitive movement in a vanishing night.

As both Ross Bullock (2005) and Naiman (1988) note, with *Happy Moscow*, Platonov approaches the theme of love, desire and happiness from a new angle and in accordance with Stalin's reversal of the early emancipatory policies.[5] It can be argued, however, that Platonov continues to thematize desire in a way that remains a serious problem for the heroes of his novels. In her urge to transmit the force of human warmth to all, Moscow enters into a conflict between private and social, particular and universal, singular and plural. As a single node of her desire to have many men, she seems unable to really be together with any one of them, and she leaves only boredom, lack of love, and loneliness behind her.[6] Impelled constantly forward by her energy, she moves from one man to another in a cycle of compensations and replacements. This is also what happens to her body, because as she challenges the circumstances of life, *Happy Moscow* becomes a story of repeated downfalls. She becomes more and more crippled, ending up lame and facing an unknown future. There is undoubtedly some criticism of the feminization of Stalinist culture here (Ross Bullock 2005), but this critique is primarily a result of the way that Platonov treats the theme of transformation in the modern world. Moscow thinks of transformation as a forward-moving actualization of energy, light, and warmth, but Platonov illustrates in her character and fate how the march from darkness to light is unable to bring about any substantial transformation of the world. The picture of modern reality conveyed by him operates according to the laws of compensation and replacement as it constantly rushes forward and spreads electrification and fire like the storm that drives Walter Benjamin's *Angelus Novus* of history:

> The angel would like to stay, awaken the dead, and make whole what has been smashed. But a storm is blowing from Paradise; it has got caught in his wings with such violence that the angel can no longer close them. The storm irresistibly propels him into the future to which his back is turned, while the pile of debris before him grows skyward. This storm is what we call progress. (Benjamin 2006, 392)

Just like the storm of progress, Moscow and the Revolution's progressive building and electrification move forcefully ahead, leaving the darkness of the world in their wake and crippling their own bodies. Platonov therefore turns to what is left behind, and in the dying echoes of Moscow's happiness pulsating in the male heroes she abandons, he shifts the focus to the world of darkness, death, desperation, and need. At the same time as he asks how the experience of the world can live on among the "unsleeping" inhabitants of modern Moscow, he turns his attention to the life-giving force of death and how it opens up a perspective on life as a locus of experience where a more profound form of sharing and transformations of desire are still possible.

ELECTRIFICATION AND A LOVE GENERATED BY LIGHT

The world in *Happy Moscow* is either transfigured or illuminated and constantly inhabited, around the clock. The beginning of this world is the night of the Revolution, when the little girl is awoken by activity lit up by a torch:

> A dark man with a burning torch was running down the street into a boring night late autumn. The little girl saw him through a window of her home as she woke from a boring dream. Then she heard the powerful shot of a rifle and a poor, sad cry—the man running with the torch had probably been killed. Soon after this came many distant shots and a din of people in the neighbouring prison . . . The girl went to sleep and forgot everything she saw later in other days: she was too small, and the memory and mind of early childhood were overgrown in her body forever by subsequent life. But until her late years a nameless man would unexpectedly and sadly rise up in her and run—the pale

light of memory—and perish once again in the dark of the past, in the heart of the grown-up child. (Platonov 2012, 7)

[Темный человек с горящим факелом бежал по улице в скучную ночь поздней осени. Маленькая девочка увидела его из окна своего дома, проснувшись от скучного сна. Потом она услышала сильный выстрел ружья и бедный грустный крик — наверно убили бежавшего с факелом человека. Вскоре послышались далекие, многие выстрелы и гул народа в ближней тюрьме . . . Девочка уснула и забыла все, что видела потом в другие дни: она была слишком мала, и память и ум раннего детства заросли в ее теле навсегда последующей жизнью. Но до поздних лет в ней неожиданно и печально поднимался и бежал безымянный человек — в бледном свете памяти — и снова погибал во тьме прошлого, в сердце выросшего ребенка.] (Platonov 2010a, 11)[7]

Again we meet the Revolution as a forgotten memory. What is characteristic of this recollection and the elemental background to the novel in general is the play between darkness and light, night and day. The light of the burning revolutionary torch is set against the background of a "boring night" and a "boring dream." The scene becomes a traumatizing memory of an illuminated night that will live on paradoxically in the girl in the "dark of the past." This image of light hiding in the gloom of memory will work in Moscow Chestnova's body as a constant impulse to change and move because

Amid hunger and sleep, at a moment of love or some young joy— suddenly the sad cry of the dead man was there again in the distance, in the depth of her body, and the young woman would immediately change her life: if she was dancing, she would interrupt the dance; if she was labouring, she would work more surely, with more concentration; if she was alone, she would cover her face with her hands. (7)

[Среди голода и сна, в момент любви или какой-нибудь молодой радости — вдруг вдалеке, в глубине тела опять раздавался грустный крик мертвого, и молодая женщина сразу меняла свою жизнь — прерывала танец, если танцевала, сосредоточенней, надежней работала, если трудилась, закрывала лицо руками, если была одна.] (11)

As she strives toward light, the memory of the Revolution takes the form of an involuntary memory that she will not be able to retrieve until she is at least more mature, yet it constantly interrupts her as the memory of another beginning. Moscow becomes fatherless and subsequently homeless at an early age. She comes under the care of the city of Moscow, whose name she is also given. Upon completing school, she leaves the orphanage. Significantly, she meets the first man to take care of her at midnight in the populated darkness of a late-night boulevard "listening to the mutterings of the thieves and homeless toughs who were standing nearby." The man, Viktor Bozhko, arranges a room for her. He as well is "unsleeping," working for nights on end answering letters and spreading the enlightening Revolution to the entire world. During the evenings in her room Moscow imagines herself as an ever-burning lamp:

> She would lean out, her stomach against the window-sill, her hair hanging down, and listen to the noise of the universal city in all its triumphant energy, and to the occasional voice that rose up from the dense and sonorous mass of mechanisms in motion; raising her head, Moscow would see the empty destitute moon rising up into the extinguished sky and she would feel inside her a warming current of life. Her imagination was continually at work and had never yet tired—in her mind she could sense the origin of matters of every kind and she took part mentally in their existence; in her solitude she filled the whole world with her attention, watching over the flames of street-lamps so they would go on shining, listening to the resounding thuds of the steam pile drivers on the Moscow River so the piles would go securely down into the depths, . . . and the conception of a better life could take place in people's ardent and firm embraces—in the dark, in privacy, face-to-face, in the pure emotion of a conjoined, doubled happiness. What Moscow wanted as not so much to experience this life as to safeguard it; she wanted to stand day and night by the brake lever of a locomotive taking people to meet another; . . . to be a lamp that goes out just at the right moment, as others kiss, taking into itself the warmth that a moment before had been light. (19)

> [Она ложилась животом на подоконник, волосы ее свисали вниз, и слушала, как шумит всемирный город в своей торжественной энергии и раздается иногда голос человека из гулкой тесноты бегущих механизмов; подняв голову, Москва видела, как восходит пустая неимущая луна на погасшее небо, и чувствовала в себе согревающее течение жизни . . . Ее воображение работало непрерывно и еще никогда не уставало, — она чувствовала в уме происхождение различных дел и мысленно принимала в них участие; в одиночестве она наполняла весь мир своим вниманием и следила за огнем фонарей, чтоб они светили, за гулкими равномерными ударами паровых копров на Москве-реке, чтоб сваи входили прочно в глубину, и думала о машинах, день и ночь напрягающихся в своей силе, чтоб горел свет в темноте, шло чтение книг, молодась рожь моторами для утреннего хлебопечения, чтоб нагнеталась вода по трубам в теплый душ танцевальных зал и происходило зачатье лучшей жизни в горячих и крепких объятиях людей — во мраке, уединении, лицом к лицу, в чистом чувстве объединенного удвоенного счастья. Москве Честновой не столько хотелось переживать самой эту жизнь, сколько обеспечивать ее — круглые сутки стоять у тормозного крана паровоза, везя людей навстречу друг другу, чинить трубу водопровода, вешать лекарства больным на аналитических весах —

и потухнуть вовремя лампой над чужим поцелуем, вберя в себя то
тепло, которое только что было светом.] (21f)

This passage presents a beautiful image of the utopian energy of the
revolutionary modernization of Moscow at work in the heroine's body
and mind. It is typical of Platonov in the way in which it shows how in
her attunement to the world her experience of herself and her body fuses
with the revolutionary discourse on electrification. Like an electric lamp
that becomes a universal source of human warmth, she wants to generate
the revolutionary promise of happiness and love for all. Very telling is
that she also wishes to "fill the whole world" with her attention, so that
the streetlamps "would go on shining," since this presupposes a world
that needs filling or compensation.[8] Indeed, she also spreads this energy
around her, and what attracts men to her is this drive toward the future
and the promise of universal happiness. Further contributing to the general atmosphere of the novel, therefore, is a later piano performance of
Beethoven's Ninth Symphony, which, like Schiller's "Ode to Joy," is an
enthusiastic and fiery expression of universal brotherhood.[9] Nevertheless, there are discordant tones throughout the novel. For example, Moscow's triumphant vision of an illuminated world with warmth for everyone is set against the background of "a destitute moon rising up into the
extinguished sky" ("pogashee nebo") (19). The past active perfective par-
ticiple of "pogasit'" underscores even more that the nocturnal luminaries
have been turned off.

Even before her ruminations on the Moscow sky, Moscow's carefree
happiness has already encountered certain obstacles to its impulse to
reach and even replace the heavens. During her very first work as a
parachutist, she attempts to light a cigarette as she dives and the para-
chute catches fire, turning her into "fireworks." She thinks to herself,
"'So, world, this is what you're really like!' . . . 'You're soft only so long as
we don't touch you!'" (18–19). The fall is the first in a series that will first
cripple and finally leave her permanently lame. Thus, Platonov shows
how the discourse on energy and electrification has determined Moscow's understanding of herself and of being in the world, and how it
leads her astray. She embodies a kind of modern "lightness of being," but
she will face the heaviness of the earth in her encounter with it. She wants
to "touch" it, but she cannot acknowledge its reciprocal contact. She is all
radiance, but she seems incapable of really experiencing anything in her
negation of darkness.

THE UNIVERSAL FORGOTTEN DREAM

The figure of the surgeon Sambikin represents a parallel to Moscow
Chestnova's obsession with the body and the idea of light and progress.
He is not caught in her irresistible net because he decides to resist the

temptation to approach her. Instead he will be the one who performs the necessary physical replacements and transfigurations after her falls. He becomes her doctor, operating on her and even doing a transplant. As a surgeon, he also serves to complement her in the way in which he probes human bodies in his search for the flow and energy of the "physical substance" of the inner life. At first, like Moscow and the others, he is haunted by the lights of the night and the constant activity that they make possible:

> At night, Sambikin took a long time to fall asleep because of the imagination of labor, now illuminated by electricity, on Soviet land. He saw structures, densely rigged with scaffolding, where unsleeping people came and went as they fastened down young boards made from fresh timber so that they themselves could remain up there, on the height where the wind blows, and from where night, in the form of the remnant of the evening glow, can be seen moving along the edge of the world. (32)

> [По ночам Самбикин долго не мог заснуть от воображения труда на советской земле, освещенного сейчас электричеством. Он видел сооружения, густо оснащенные тесом, где ходили неспящие люди, укрепляя молодые доски из свежего леса, чтобы самим держаться на высоте, где дует ветер и видно; как идет ночь по краю мира в виде остатка вечерней зари.] (30)

Through Sambikin and in his ruminations, Platonov further develops the problem of a world intent on acquiring electricity and light. The mere image of the constantly illuminated and constantly working country with its "unsleeping" people keeps Sambikin from falling asleep.[10] Besides his work as a surgeon, which keeps him busy to the point of exhaustion, he also cannot stop thinking "constantly and without interruption" (34) about the transformation of the world. Because of his scientific fervor, he only has daydreams—dreams at night torment him, and he sleeps without resting. Intellectually, he is concerned with the future of the substance of the world. Like Voshchev, who digs into the earth for the truth about existence, Sambikin digs into human bodies and explores the human substance for an answer to the meaning of life and the course of the world. Presented in a kind of dark humor, however, he is one of the few characters in Platonov's novels who actually reaches some sort of insight into life. He recognizes the limitations of his analytic activity and realizes that like the Revolution for Dvanov, the human understanding also resembles a forgotten dream:

> he immediately realized how much a human being is still a feebly constructed, homespun being—no more than a vague embryo and blueprint of something more authentic— and how much work must be done to unfurl from this the embryo the flying higher image buried in our dream. (35)

[он тут же понял, насколько человек еще самодельное, немощно устроенное существо — не более, как смутный зародыш и проект чего-то более действительного, и сколько надо еще работать, чтобы развернуть из этого зародыша летящий, высший образ, погребенный в вашей мечте.] (36)

In a phrasing that is very reminiscent of Voschev's thoughts as he digs into the earth that "he would need to possess life for a long time in order to overcome, by means of oblivion and labor, this embedded world that had hidden in its own darkness the truth of all existence," Sambikin asserts that "much work must be done to unfurl . . . the embryo . . . buried in our dream." In other words, he realizes that there in the body, or rather in the dream, is concealed another "image," a "blueprint of something more authentic." This leads him to abandon his obsession with light and day, and to want to sleep. He does not give up his scientific activity, however, and unlike Voshchev, who does not find an answer in the earth, the material of the body will give him an explanation. He, at least, thinks that he finds "the reason for all life" in between emptiness and excrements:

"This heart too bears traces of the unknown secretion I was telling you about," Sambikin informed his friend. "Death, when it rushes through the body, breaks the seal on that clenched life lying in reserve—and then, like an unsuccessful shot, life resounds inside a person for the last time and leaves unclear traces on his dead heart. But that substance, in terms of its energy, is supremely precious. It's very strange—what's most vital of all appears at the moment of the last breath." (62)

[На этом сердце тоже есть следы той неизвестной секреции, о которой я тебе говорил, — сообщил Самбикин своему другу. — Смерть, когда она несется по телу, срывает печать с запасной, сжатой жизни и она раздается внутри человека в последний раз, как безуспешный выстрел, и оставляет неясные следы на его мертвом сердце . . . Но это вещество — высшая драгоценность по своей энергии. И странно, самое живое появляется в момент последнего дыхания.] (60)

This substance, also called the soul, is found between food and excrements. Consequently, Sambikin understands that "the world consisted primarily of destitute substance, which it was almost impossible to love but essential to understand" (64). Again, Platonov draws our attention to life as an in-between. The dark humor of this discovery also marks a crucial change of perspective in both the novel and the characters. Instead of experiencing the world from the viewpoint of Moscow Chestnova's relation to the world as she restlessly rushes to the brightness of the future, we are now invited to look at the world from the viewpoint of the soul as an empty void, a destitute, abject substance. From this angle, which is opposite of that taken by the storm of progress, life as well will appear entirely different. Indeed, as Platonov suggests, it is the perspective from which life will appear as life, because it is not understood in its projection.

THE LIFE OF THE EXTINGUISHED NIGHT: TRANSFORMATION INTO THE OTHER

Moscow herself becomes more and more crippled, and her lovers are increasingly sorrowful and deserted. They also come to open another dimension of the world. Her most infatuated lover is the engineer Sartorius, who is also entirely swept up by the discourse on energy. In his desperation after she leaves him, however, he also embarks upon an entirely different course in life. Toward the end of her life, Moscow decides to marry the reservist Komyagin, who unlike Sartorius and Sambikin, has no inclination to think. After a rather hideous scene next to what is erroneously assumed to be Komyagin's corpse, Moscow and Sartorius revive their love. He turns to contemplate the city outside:

> Sartorius took fright: all that had been allotted to him, out of the entire world, was one warm drop stored in his breast, and he might never sense what remained but lie down soon in a corner like Komyagin. His heart seemed to turn dark but he comforted it with an ordinary understanding that came to his mind: that it was necessary to research the entire extent of current life through the transformation of himself into others . . . he intended to use events and circumstances to annihilate the resistance of his personality, so that the unknown feelings of others could enter him one by one. (100)

> [Сарториус испугался, что ему изо всего мира досталась лишь одна теплая капля, хранимая в груди, а остального он не почувствует и скоро ляжет в угол, подобно Комягину. Сердце его стало как темное, но он утешил его обыкновенным понятием, пришедшим ему в ум, что нужно исследовать весь объем текущей жизни посредством превращения себя в прочих людей. Сарториус погладил свое тело по сторонам, обрекая его перемучиться на другое существование, которое запрещено законом природы и привычкой человека к самому себе. Он был исследователем и не берег себя для тайного счастья, а сопротивление своей личности предполагал уничтожить событиями и обстоятельствами, чтобы по очереди могли в него войти неизвестные чувства других людей. Раз появился жить, нельзя упустить этой возможности, необходимо вникнуть во все посторонние души — иначе ведь некуда деться; с самим собою жить нечем, и кто так живет, тот погибает задолго до гроба /можно только вытаращить глаза и обомлеть от идиотизма.] (94f)

Having discovered life beyond himself, Sartorius undergoes a conversion. He is as if released from the idea of self-fulfilment and therefore ready to take on the suffering of others.[11] It is with such feelings that he goes to the graveyard to watch over and remember the dead. It is also in this frame of mind that he in fact enters into the sort of transformative process portrayed in Arnold Schönberg's string sextet, "Transfigured Night."[12] In the poem behind the music the lyrical I discovers during a moonlit walk that his beloved is pregnant with a child from another man, but he comforts her that she must not worry, the child will become like his own, because "a special warmth flickers from me to you, from you to me." Sartorius first transfigures himself by adopting the name and identity of the deceased Grunyakhin, who is "the second person of his life" (110). To acquire a family and some human warmth, he further decides to move in with the destitute and desperate Matryona Fillipovna and her sons.

There is a Christological theme in Sartorius's transformation into another person when confronted by the need of the other. He undoubtedly shoulders the other's yoke. He does not so much leave one self and assume another as he abandons the very idea of the self. It is not necessarily puritanical, but it favors a different universality than the universal love that Moscow Chestnova seeks to spread. His family is also not what they seem to be, and the novel ends:

> At night, after his wife and son had gone to sleep, Semyon Ivanovich would stand there, above Matryona Filippovna's face, and observe how entirely helpless she was, how pathetically her face had clenched in miserable exhaustion, while her eyes closed like kind eyes, as if, while she lay unconscious, some ancient angel were resting in her. If all of humanity were lying still and sleeping, it would be impossible to judge its real character from its face and one could be deceived. (117)

> [Ночью, когда жена и сын уснули, Иван Степанович стоял над лицом Матрены Филипповны и наблюдал, как она вся беспомощна, как жалобно было сжато ее лицо в тоскливой усталости и глаза были закрыты как добрые, точно в ней, когда она лежала без сознания, покоился древний ангел. Если бы все человечество лежало спящим, то по лицу его нельзя было бы узнать его настоящего характера и можно было бы обмануться.] (110)

The last sentence is tricky, and it carries more than it may first seem to hold. For the difference between man's appearance in a waking state and while asleep is not only the difference between what man *is* and what he seems to be, but also suggests that man perhaps *is not* what he is, and that this is manifested in the face of the sleeper. Platonov asserts that we would probably not be able to read the "real character"—or "nastoiashchii kharakter"—which can also be translated as "real qualities"—on the face of all of humanity in its sleep. Notably, in the Russian original, "all of humanity" ("vsë chelovechestvo") has the form of one subject and it governs the predicate in the singular form "lezhalo." This serves to emphasize universality as a common being that in sleep lacks face and is really not what it seems in active, waking moments. Platonov thus suggests not only that man encompasses an infinite alterity or difference due to his hidden universality, but also that man is other to himself, and that the night and sleep are where this other, as the remains of an ancient angel, can be retrieved. Platonov does not think of this other self as a superego or truer self, but simply as the way that the self is inhabited by others, just like the tenants of the building guarded by the eunuch in *Chevengur*.

Happy Moscow is a parable about the flawed modern belief in universal salvation through progress, with a particular focus on electrification as the source of light and warmth both in the concrete sense of lighting in the home and in the streets and in the sense of enlightenment of the hearts and the minds of the people. In her rush forward and urge for transformation, Moscow spreads love and warmth, but at the same time she is in need of no one and unable to account for the touch of the other. Sartorius follows an inverse evolution, transforming himself through the memory of the dead and rejected. He takes upon himself the identity of a dead man and joins his family, replacing the deceased father who was rejected by "his sons." Similarly, instead of discovering light and love as a life-giving element, Sambikin discovers death to be the source of life.[13]

What really worries Platonov in Moscow Chestnova's imaginations of happiness is the disappearing loci of true darkness in the illuminated and full inner and outer life. The problem in both *Happy Moscow* and the modern world is that this night has been extinguished and is always inhabited and illuminated. The modern world is transfiguring and transforming everything—including its loci of negativity, by making it manifest in light. The only disappearance and transformation that can take place is a disappearance into the crowd, into further meetings and transformations into sameness. Thus *Happy Moscow* moves from an "Ode to Joy" to an apologia for sleep and a kind of "Ode to the Night." Like Novalis, Platonov suggests that it is the darkness of night rather than the light of day that is the locus of love and happiness. As opposed to the outer changes represented by light and electrification, the night is the locus of inner transformations and transfigurations.[14] This is evident from Komyagin's poem dedicated to the night:

> In that night, O in that night, the sleep of field and farm
> was light;
> Paths called out to them in silence, stretching out toward
> a star,
> And the steppe in languor breathing, bare of body, quiet
> of heart,
> Seemed to stand in fear upon a trembling bridge that
> floated far. (65)

[– А истина полагается пролетариату? спросил Вощев.

– Пролетариату полагается движение, – произнес активист, а что навстречу попадается, то все его: будь там истина, будь кулацкая награбленная кофта – все пойдет в организованный котел, ты ничего не узнаешь!] (477)

Platonov depicts the night, when we seem to fall into our bodies, as the time when we also abandon our bodies as ourselves. In the sleep of the night there is another lightness, "bare of body, quiet of heart," where another distance speaks, as "the bridge/ that floated far." Thus for Platonov the night offers a possibility to access what is distant and different, whereas the day and the light are the realm of sameness, whatever it may be.

NOTES

1. Cf. Kostov (2000, 80); Kornienko (1999, 581).

2. Sandomirskaja develops her reading of word happiness in *Happy Moscow* into an interesting argument about the relation between happiness and general economy in a comparison of Platonov and Bataille.

3. See for instance, Barsht (2003) and Sandomirskaja (2017).

4. References below to this edition are by page number only

5. Both Ross Bullock and Naiman see a sort of failed attempt to break with the puritan brotherhood of Platonov's early works because here he fails to embrace desire and the "feminization" of culture.

6. Cf. Günther (2011, 165), who writes, "Сцены телесной близости подтверждают роль пола как компенсации непреодолимого одиночества людей. Все эмоциональные, духовные ценности растворяются в физиологических деталях" ["The scenes of physical intimacy confirm the role of sex as compensation for insurmountable loneliness. All emotional and spiritual values dissolve in physiological details."]

7. References to this edition below are by page number only.

8. Günther (2011, 165) develops an in-depth reading of this theme.

9. See also Bullock (2004, 54f.).

10. Cf. Sá Cavalcante Schuback (2017).

11. "Life's fundamental obligation—concern over one's personal fate, the sense of one's own body, constantly crying out with feelings—had disappeared. He could not go on being the same uninterrupted person; a yearning was beginning in him" (105).

12. Schönberg's "Verklärte Nacht" is inspired by a poem by Richard Dehmel that treats the theme of a secondary love. When the lyrical "I" realizes that his love has been unfaithful and is pregnant with the child of another man, he takes this love upon himself.

13. At the same time, Platonov approaches the question of singularity and plurality in relation to communality as developed, for instance, by Agamben in *The Coming Community* and Nancy in *Being Singular Plural*. Agamben insists on singularity and hence also on universality based on the notion of the "whatever" (*quodlibet*) as the name that which escapes the pitfalls of identity and therefore lacks a name as an empty space. The "whatever" is the "figure of pure singularity" (67). It is in other words also an attempt to find an ontological ground for a new idea of communality after the fall of Communism, which had proven to be but a common identity. In a way, Platonov seems to confirm Agamben's idea of the singularity of the subject beyond identity based on the whatever, when he turns Sambikin precisely into a "whatever": a person able to be anybody at all and to enter different lives and take upon himself

different identities. Yet for Platonov, the "whatever" of the awakened world only reflects the more originary distinction between sleep and waking. In sleep, man is something else, but this something else is not a substance or essence, but an opening to the transformations of the world in the self.

14. Cf. Novalis (2013) who writes about "zahllose Verwandlungen."

FIVE

Dzhan

Retrieving the Inner

Like *The Foundation Pit*, the novella *Dzhan* (translated into English as *Soul*) has a conceptual structure. Thanks to Gorky, Platonov was among the writers invited to go to Central Asia to testify to the building of socialism in the Soviet republics. On the occasion of the ten-year anniversary of Turkmenistan in early 1934, he was sent in a writers' brigade to study and chronicle the success of this Soviet project. More than discovering the triumph of Soviet civilization, however, Platonov gained an insight into the life of the poor natives of the region. In a letter dated April 15, 1934, he describes an excursion to the desert as follows:

> We stayed until the first stars appeared. The desert made an enormous impression on me. I understood something that I had not understood before.
>
> [Мы были до первых звезд. Пустыня произвела на меня огромное впечатление. Я кое-что понял, чего раньше не понимал.] (Platonov 2013, 357)

As Robert Chandler (2003, 48) notes, Platonov felt at home in the ascetic way of life in Central Asia and returned early the next year. In January 1935, in Turkmenistan, he began to write *Dzhan,* a narrative about the discovery of a home and a greatness that differs from what is appreciated in modern society. The plot revolves around the economist Nazar Chagataev, who is sent from Moscow to rescue the starving Dzhan people on the Kirghyz-Uzbek border by leading them to the valley of Ust-Urt, where Soviet civilization can help take care of them. Characteristically, however, Platonov inverts the relationship between the savior and the saved, so that when the people arrive in Ust-Urt they find themselves

91

"lost" in civilization, and Chagataev, in contrast, has "gained" an insight into a new sensitivity in his life among the poor natives. What is more, it seems that somewhere around the time of the writing of *Dzhan,* Platonov turns his focus from the problems of the realization of a revolutionary community according to the official party line in society to the question of desire and the experience of inner life as a locus of the revolutionary experience of the world. Chagataev and the Dzhan's biblical trek through the desert is on a superficial level presented as a journey from the provinces to the city, from destitute poverty to socialism, from hunger to well-being; or, as a party secretary in the novel puts it, a journey from hell to paradise. The physical survival of the Dzhan (a Persian word that Platonov deciphers as meaning "soul" or "dear little life") is pitted against the endurance of the Inner, for when the Dzhan reach civilization they lose the richness of their experience of the world.

Dzhan symbolizes one of the most fundamental political myths of the twentieth century, namely the story of how the other, a foreign people, is received and adopted into the redemptive communion of civilization. It is the myth of the transfer and incorporation of the outside, of negativity, and of losers, into the success story of modern society, where life abounds in happiness. Platonov follows the schema of this myth and its implementation in the project of building the Soviet republics, but in the end he undermines it. Although Chagataev does indeed shepherd the people from starvation to food, from the desert in the mountains to a verdant valley and from poverty to plenty, he does not lead them to salvation. On the contrary, in the civilized world they lose their communality and become fragmented and estranged from each other. With the loss of the commonality of poverty they also lose *dzhan*: "the dear little life."[1]

THE LOST PEOPLE OF *DZHAN*

Although the title *Dzhan* denotes a people and thus suggests kinship, nowhere in the novel itself is there any such sense of belonging or home in relation to either a people or a space. To begin with, Nazar Chagataev "stems" from the people in the sense that his mother is a Dzhan and he was born and initially raised among them before she sent him away to escape starvation through adoption into the so-called Great Soviet Family in Moscow, where he also received his education. While his life in Moscow is characterized by estrangement and a constant preoccupation with ephemeral pleasures,[2] it might seem that by going to the Dzhan and Central Asia Chagataev "returns" to the people that he has lost—to the own, or to his self. The Dzhan, however, are not a people in any original or positive sense. They are "a people who have forgotten who they are" (23) and do not provide any ground or sense of belonging. In a conversation with Chagataev upon his arrival in Tashkent, the party secretary calls them a "lost nation,"[3] because they are not rooted in their surroundings but have been forced to move there. And when the party secretary asks: "Did your mother ever tell you who the Dzhan are?" Chagataev answers:

> She did. She said that they were runaways and orphans from everywhere, and old, exhausted slaves who had been cast out. There were women who had betrayed their husbands and then vanished, fleeing to Sary-Kamysh in fear. There were young girls who came and never left because they loved men who had suddenly died and they didn't want to marry anyone else. And people who didn't know God, people who mocked the world. There were criminals. But I was only a little boy—I can't remember them all. (24)

> [Беглецы и сироты отовсюду и старые изнемогшие рабы, которых прогнали. Потом были женщины, изменившие мужьям и попавшие туда от страха, приходили навсегда девушки, полюбившие тех, кто вдруг умер, а они не захотели никого другого в мужья. И еще там жили люди, не знающие бога, насмешники над миром, преступники . . .] (131)

This "lost nation" or "lost people" is a collection of worthless slaves, criminals, adulterers, and persons who have not known "God." They have been "in hell," and Chagataev's task is to lead them to paradise:

> Your nation has already been in hell. Now let it live in paradise for a while—and we'll help it with all our strength. You will be our representative. (24)

> [В аду твой народ уже был, пусть поживет в раю, а мы ему поможем всей нашей силой . . . Ты будешь нашим уполномоченным.] (131)

The biblical connotations are obvious: the people are to be taken from hell to heaven, a journey that involves a trek through the desert. Also, as the people themselves are called "Dzhan," meaning "soul" or "dear life," who have "only their hearts," "only life itself," we can tentatively suggest that it is the salvation of the soul and life that is somehow at stake here. Because of its parable-like narrative structure and many allusions to and ruminations on otherworldly aspects of being, Slavic scholars have in fact linked *Dzhan* to several myths.[4] Early in the novel, Chagataev repeatedly reflects on life in relation to eternity. For instance, he considers a picture depicting the duality of existence by Camille Flammarion on the wall in his Moscow wife Vera's room. This picture, however, seems first and foremost to resound in the existential dualism between outer movement and inner memory that is central to the story. In my reading, *Dzhan* tells a paradoxical tale in which the journey to paradise to save these poor lost souls, or the soul of the Dzhan, is at the same time a failure and results in the loss of the experience of life that the people of Dzhan exemplify. The Dzhan cannot be retrieved and transferred to civilization from this "hell." "Dzhan," or "dear little life," stands for a communality experienced inwardly in extreme situations of physical deprivation. Chagataev does not understand this on a conscious level, but when asleep he senses that there is a different kind of greatness to this people:

> He was smiling. Everything in this existing world seemed strange to him; it was as if the world had been created for some brief, mocking game. But this game of make-believe had dragged on for a long time, for eternity, and nobody felt like laughing any more. The desert's deserted emptiness, the camel, even the pitiful wandering grass—all this ought to be serious, grand and triumphant. Inside every poor creature was a sense of some other happy destiny, a destiny that was necessary and inevitable—why, then, did they find their lives such a burden and why were they always waiting for something? Chagataev curled up against the camel's stomach and fell asleep, full of astonishment at strange reality. (27f.)

> [Он улыбался; все было странно для него в этом существующем мире, сделанном как будто для краткой насмешливой игры. Но эта нарочная игра затянулась надолго, на вечность, и смеяться никто уже не хочет, не может. Пустая земля пустыни, верблюд, даже бродячая жалкая трава — ведь это все должно быть серьезным, великим и торжествующим; внутри бедных существ есть чувство их другого, счастливого назначения, необходимого и непременного, — зачем же они так тяготятся и ждут чего-то? Чагатаев свернулся калачом около живота верблюда и уснул, удивляясь необыкновенной действительности.] (134)

In contrast to the promise of future happiness, Chagataev senses "another destination" that belongs to these "poor beings" ("bednykh sushchestv") and to the poor as such. The Dzhan have nothing but themselves, or, as Chagataev states elsewhere, they have "only life itself . . . But even life wasn't really their own" (24) ("odna tol'ko zhizn. . . No i zhizn' byla ne ego") (131). This other destination is the sense of life as "serious, grand and triumphant," and it is contrasted with the experience of life as a joke that has become tedious and burdensome. The strength of this people, their other destination, lies in the "destiny that was necessary and inevitable." In their poor life, everything they come across—people, things, memories—is present as an inevitable necessity, which ultimately means that unlike Chagataev's civilized world, where a kind of absence lies over everything, what these people surround themselves with is present to them. Through the Dzhan, Chagataev begins to sense the meaning of necessity and inevitability, but this insight comes to him only in the amazement he experiences on the edge of slumber or in extreme situations on the boundary of life and death.

THE RETURN IN THE DEPARTURE

Instead of a myth portraying how the other, the strange, and the distant becomes the own, the intimate and the common, Platonov's story tells us that the own is strange and foreign, and that the foreign and strange is the own. Not only is Dzhan not really a nation lost and forgotten, even to themselves, but there is also no apparent pattern to their movements. The narrative, which at first sight seems to depict the transfer or departure of a people from a place with a life and a world and their arrival in civilization, also tells us that we are never able either to leave or to arrive. Platonov shows us a people living in constant forgetfulness of things and life around them, perpetually oblivious of their own being and the being of the other.

As often in Platonov's works, the opening presents the significant existential legend that he is about to tell. Here we are immediately introduced to a scene that bespeaks our sense of alienation and forgetfulness of presence in the world. *Dzhan* begins as Nazar Chagataev, who "is not a Russian" — in other words, a stranger — "leaves" or "goes out" into the courtyard of the institute where he is studying:

> Into the courtyard of the Moscow Institute of Economics walked a young man who was not a Russian, Nazar Chagataev. He looked around in surprise and came back to himself from the long time that had passed. He had crossed this yard again and again over the years; it was in these buildings that his youth had gone by, but he felt no regret. He had climbed up high no, onto the mountain of his mind, and from there he had a clearer view of the whole of this summer world, now warmed by an evening sun that had had its day. (3)

> [Во двор Московского экономического института вышел молодой нерусский человек Назар Чагатаев. Он с удивлением осмотрелся кругом и опомнился от минувшего долгого времени. Здесь, по этому двору, он ходил несколько лет, и здесь прошла его юность, но он не жалеет о ней, — он взошел теперь высоко, на гору своего ума, откуда виднее весь этот летний мир, нагретый вечерним отшумевшим солнцем.] (113)

What this first paragraph tells us is that time will be an important theme in the novel. The whole scene breathes an atmosphere of the past — Chagataev has finished his studies and is greeted by an evening sun that "had had its day." As he gazes around after completing his studies, however, he goes out into the world in the present, in order to "come to himself" ("opomnilsia"). His usual world was strange: he looked at it "with surprise" ("s udivleniem") in a moment of rediscovery or a kind of awakening, not after, but *from* "the long time that had passed." He does not see this forgotten world until the moment he takes leave of it; indeed, leaving it seems to be the basis for his discovery of what was. At this moment of departure, Chagataev wishes to linger in this world of "dead things" that hopefully will someday come to life. He touches all things in what appears to be a vain farewell gesture, knowing that soon they will also forget him. The strangeness of the world applies not only to the world, but also to people. He meets Vera, who in the beginning appeals to him as if from a distance:

> This temporary stranger, this woman he would probably never meet again, gave off a sense of sleep and happiness; thus it is that bliss often lives unnoticed by us. (7)

> [Сон и счастье исходили от этой чужой женщины, с которой он, вероятно, не встретится более; так часто живет рядом с нами незаметное блаженство.] (116)

Thus, Platonov describes a world in which things and beings live unaware of each other. Chagataev laments this atmosphere of collective oblivion. He desires recognition from the objects with which he surrounds himself, but most often he is an "unknown and pitiful creature" in their presence. He encounters this same obliviousness upon his arrival in Tashkent:

> Feeling hurt, he walked as if through a foreign world, staring at everything around him and recognizing things he had forgotten, though still going unrecognized himself. It seemed as though every little creature, object or plant was prouder, more independent of former attachment, than a human being. (26)

> [Он шел обиженный, как по чужому миру, вглядываясь во все окружающее и узнавая забытое, но сам оставался неузнанным. Каждое мелкое существо, предмет и растение, оказывается, было более гордым и независимым от прежней привязанности, чем человек.] (133)

Parallel to his lack of a sense of presence in Moscow and Tashkent, and later in the desert of Sary-Kamysh, Chagataev very keenly senses the estrangement that his own past absence in that world creates. Upon returning to the places of his childhood, he focuses "the interest of memory" (22) on the world, but recognizes that there is no place for nostalgia because there is no place for him in its memory. The world he walks around in is strange because it does not recognize him. All that he encounters are the absence and the distance that have come between him and his childhood surroundings. The only things that are aware of him are some old bushes:

> His mother had once led him here by the hand and sent him off to live on his own, and now he had come back. He walked on with the camel, into the heart of his native land. Wild bushes stood there like wizened old men. They had not grown since Chagataev's childhood and they alone of all the living creatures around appeared not to have forgotten

Chagataev; they were so very unattractive as to seem meek and it was impossible to believe they could be indifferent or forgetful. Hideously poor as they were, they could keep going only with the help of memory or the lives of others; there was no other way they could live. (28)

[Сюда его мать когда-то вывела за руку и отправила жить одного, а теперь он вернулся. Он пошел дальше с верблюдом, в середину родины. Как маленькие старики, стояли дикие кустарники; они не выросли с тех пор, когда Чагатаев был ребенком, и они, кажется, одни из всех местных существ не забыли Чагатаева, потому что были настолько непривлекательны, что это походило на кротость, и в равнодушие или в беспамятство их поверить было нельзя. Такие безобразные бедняки должны жить лишь воспоминанием или чужой жизнью, больше им нечем.] (134f.)

Insensitive indifference and forgetfulness are features that do not apply to these wretched bushes, for it is "only with the help of memory or the lives of others" that they can go on living. It is the world of necessity that determines the specific sensitivity of the poor. Chagataev does not have this sensitivity because he consumes encounters with others as ephemeral and temporary, much as he would ingest something edible. When the old man Sufyan tells Chagataev that he knows him, and Chagataev replies that he cannot remember him, Sufyan explains:

You don't know me, because you live like you eat. What goes into you, comes out again later. But what's inside me, remains there. (30)

[Ты не знаешь, ты живешь, как ешь: что в тебя входит, то потом выходит. А во мне, все задерживается.] (136)

The comparison of life and food points to why the poor sense another destination in life. Platonov suggests that there is a deeper parallel between devouring victuals and the consumption of people. We take both "into" our Inner—food in a material form and people figuratively as memories—but when we overconsume both food and people, we no longer feel what we are consuming and cease to be aware of the other in ourselves. Food immediately leaves Chagataev, but it stays a while ("zaderzhivaetsia") in the poor man.[5] Indeed, Platonov's definition of overconsumption is when man ceases to feel the other in himself, and this is also why Chagataev's initial task of saving the Dzhan is doomed to fail, for leading them to abundance means leading them to forgetfulness. In Sary-Kamish, from which Chagataev sets off on this journey, therefore, there is no bread in the physical sense, but at the end point in Ust-Urt, and later in Moscow there is an opposite lack of spiritual bread, because people have stopped experiencing "the memory of lives of the other."

Indeed, the feeling of the immaterial Inner is the strange experience that his travels will bring to him, but it is an experience that he finds difficult to take with him from the journey across the desert. In the desert under conditions of physical starvation, when the "usual world" is replaced by a dreamlike experience, the world makes itself accessible to experience in a more exposed form:

> Sufyan understood that Chagataev was being agitated by some kind of vital excitement, but this did not interest him. He knew that a man has to fill up his soul with something other and that, if there's nothing at all, the heart ends up greedily chewing its own blood. After four days Sufyan and Chagataev were so hungry that they began to see dreams, even though their legs were walking and their eyes saw ordinary day. (36)

> [Суфьян понимал, что в Чагатаеве происходит сейчас какое-то волнение жизни, но не интересовался этим: он знал, что чем-нибудь надо человеку наполнять свою душу, и если нет ничего, то сердце алчно жует собственную кровь. Через четыре дня Суфьян и Чагатаев настолько захотели есть, что стали видеть сновидения, в то время как ноги их шли и глаза видели обыкновенный день.] (141)

In this story of the road from starvation to salvation, Platonov turns the concepts of physical and spiritual nourishment and satisfaction on their heads. What Chagataev needs appears to be not so much food as other people, or rather, the recognition of their presence as memories in himself. Yet this is what the desert trek will bring to him, because in such a state of minimum energy the appearance of the individual self is less, and this increases the experience of the others in oneself. And as we shall see, experiencing others in the self is the definition of "dear little life" in Platonov's ontology.

THE DESERT TREK AND THE APPEARANCE OF THE OTHER

The journey through the desert is a great trial for Chagataev and the Dzhan. For days they find no food, and one child dies and simply vanishes in the sand and is forgotten. Life in the desert is reduced to a minimum. Verging on nonbeing, it will offer to Chagataev an experience of life in entropic fullness on the border of death. The Dzhan follow him, moving slowly and silently through the desert and feeding on whatever living vegetation they can find. Sometimes they walk, sometimes they crawl. An intrigue develops, however, because of Nur-Muhammed, an envoy from the party who was sent to the people before Chagataev. He is a selfish man who does not understand this people and constantly serves only himself. At one point, he lusts for Aidym, a little girl who is attached to Chagataev. When Nazar defends her, Nur-Muhammed shoots him. Wounded, he falls behind and is separated from the people. He crawls along, feeding on dry branches and grass. In this condition of utter exhaustion and as he sleeps, he finds within himself a relationship with the memory of other people:

Chagataev crawled another few yards and, in shallow, sandy tombs, found some dried-up blades of spring grass; these too he swallowed, just as he found them. After sliding down from a dune, he fell asleep at its base, and in sleep his weak consciousness was attacked by all kinds of memories: aimless, forgotten impressions, images of dull faces he had once happened to see—the whole of his past life suddenly turned back and fell on Chagataev. A poor, elderly man, someone he had once talked to somewhere or other, in Moscow or in his childhood, entered Chagataev's mind and was now muttering away there about who knows what, never coming to an end and not going away. (73)

[Затем Чагатаев пополззал еще по окрестности в несколько шагов и нашел в мелких песчаных могилах весенние засохшие былинки травы, которые он также проглотил, без различия. Скатившись с бархана, он заснул у его подножия, и во сне на его слабое сознание напали разные воспоминания, бесцельные забытые впечатления, воображение скучных лиц, виденных когда-то, однажды, — вся прожитая жизнь вдруг повернулась назад и напала на Чагатаева. Вот бедный пожилой человек, с которым говорил где-то Чагатаев, не то в Москве, не то в детстве, вошел к нему в ум и бормотал неизвестно о чем, не кончая и не уходя.] (173)

As he lies in the sand on the verge of death, a dream gives him access to forgotten memories: "the whole of his life suddenly turned back and fell on Chagataev." In this semiconscious half-being, his entire life opens itself to him as a memory in himself beyond any important or valuable meeting or events:

Earlier he had thought that most of the unimportant, and even the not so unimportant, episodes of his life had been forgotten forever, eternally overshadowed by subsequent major events, but now he realized that all these things were intact inside him, indestructible, as perfectly preserved as precious treasures, as the possessions of a rapacious beggar who hoards what no one needs and what others have thrown away. The poor, elderly, man did not disappear from Chagataev's consciousness; there he was, still muttering something, begging or complaining (in reality he had probably died long ago), but now a friend of Vera's someone he had once barely glimpsed, had bent down over Chagataev and she wouldn't go away either, she was annoying him, her whole being was tormenting the man half-asleep in the desert, while behind her, on a clay wall, trembled shadows from a silvery branch that had once grown in the sun, perhaps in Chardzhou or somewhere else. (73f.)

[Раньше он думал, что большинство ничтожных и даже важных событий его жизни забыто навсегда, закрыто навечно последующим крупными фактами, — сейчас он понял, что в нем все цело, неуничтожимо и сохранно, как драгоценность, как добро хищного нищего, который бережет ненужное и брошенное другими. Бедный и пожилой человек не исчез из сознания, он все еще бормотал что-то, прося или жалуясь (наверное, он давно умер в действительности), но вот подруга Веры, еле виденная им когда-то, склонилась над Чагатаевым и не уходила, она надоедала, и она мучила собою дремлющего в пустыне человека, и за нею, на глиняном дувале, дрожали тени от серебристой ветви, росшей некогда на солнце — может быть, в Чарджуе, может быть, еще где-нибудь.] (173)

Platonov emphasizes the existence of the unimportant and worthless in us that extends beyond the ramifications of any ordinary conscious-ness of reality. A man who in Chagataev's more conscious memory has no status or place makes his presence suddenly felt. Thus, Chagataev comes to understand that all people and things he meets live on in him beyond his conscious will. He discovers that in his Inner "the rejected and abandoned" is as "valuable and well-kept as a jewel." Indeed, he discovers that his inner self is a "rapacious beggar who hoards what no one needs and what others have thrown away." Thus, all hierarchies of reality (and realism) in the Inner are inverted in extreme poverty and on the borders of consciousness. This beautiful passage continues:

> And there were many other pungent, eternal bits of empty piffle: a rotten tree, a village post-office, a deserted mountain groaning in the midday sun, the sounds of a disappeared wind and of tender embraces with Vera—all these things entered Chagataev energetically and simul-taneously and then continued to live inside him, motionless and persis-tent, even though in reality, in the past, they had been current facts that had slipped quickly by and vanished. They now existed more sharply and fiercely inside him, much more insistently than they had ever ex-isted before. In real life these things had lived meekly, they had not proclaimed their significance and had done no harm to man's con-science and feelings. But now they had all come crowding into Chaga-taev's head and, whereas in the real world it had been possible to escape from them, if only because time goes on passing, now these events had nowhere to slip away to; now they went on being and being, eating at the bones of Chagataev's skull and wearing them away with all this repetition. (74)

> [И еще многие, едкие вечные пустяки в виде сгнившего дерева, почтового отделения в поселке, безлюдной стонущей горы на полуденном солнце, звука пропавшего ветра и нежных объятий с Верой, все это энергично вошло в Чагатаева одновременно и жило в нем неподвижно и настойчиво, хотя в истине, в прошлом, это были текущие, быстро исчезающие факты. В нем же они теперь существовали гораздо более резко и яростно, гораздо навязчивей, чем на правде. В действительности эти предметы жили кротко и не проявляли своего значения, не делали больно совести и чувству человека. Но сейчас они набились толпою в голову Чагатаева, и если от них можно было спасаться в настоящей жизни, хотя бы потому, что время проходит, то здесь события никуда не проходили, а продолжали быть постоянно и своей

повторяющейся деятельностью точили и протирали кости черепа
Чагатаева.] (173f.)

Chagataev thought he could consume other people just as quickly as
he consumed his food. The series of women that he has met ultimately
become as estranged from him as the world that he constantly leaves
behind. It is in the in-between, in the journey through the desert, on the
borders of existence, that he understands how wrong he has been. He
begins to feel how he consists of his memory, indeed, how the world of
spirit or the soul awakens in him. What exists in him exists in contradic-
tion to "reality," where everything appears as "ephemeral and rapidly
vanishing facts." In real life everything that he had met could enter into a
relationship of meanings and values where they did not "do any harm to
human feelings and the human consciousness." In dreams, as in a dream
on the border of life and death, reality lives in another intimate form in
us.

Here on the boundary of waking and sleep, consciousness and unconsciousness, life and death, Chagataev experiences that which cannot fully
appear in life or consciousness: the other in the self. Thus, Platonov tells
us that man does not have a home in the world, in the sense that he does
not inhabit the world as a home, but that man himself is a home for the
world and is inhabited by it. He experiences how we are the other in us,
and how on the verge of death we feel the presence of everything living
in us that is strange, rejected, worthless, and forgotten. Platonov also
inverts the traditional Western notion of the soul, according to which it is
the uttermost own, equally the basis of the Delphic motto, "know thy-
self," the Aristotelian self-mover, and the Christian road to salvation. For
Platonov, however, the soul is the immaterial presence of the other in the
self. The soul or "dear little life" is the way in which, contrary to consciousness and reality, the world persists as a common remembered relationship in our Inner.

THE MEMORY OF THE DZHAN PEOPLE

Although the Dzhan are described from the outset as a "lost nation,"
toward the end of the novella they lose themselves in a different sense.
Their arrival in the valley of Ust-Urt, is but the beginning of the story of
their dispersal, disappearance, and alienation. Aidym senses this. As they
reach their goal, she turns to Chagataev and asks,

> "Teach me not to think. I am frightened. I see terrible things," said
> Aidym.
> "But it's not hunger that's hurting your soul, is it?" asked Chaga-
> taev.
> "No," said Aidym. My soul's hurting from what I feel. Nazar, why
> doesn't anyone need me?

"Who doesn't need you?" asked Chagataev.

The nation was living with us, and now it's just wandered off," said Aidym. "Soon you'll leave too. Who'll be left to remember me then?"

"I won't leave you," Chagataev promised. (121)

["Научи меня, чтоб я лучше не думала, а то я боюсь: мне кажется страшное!" сказала Айдым.

"Но ведь у тебя не от голода душа начинает болеть?" спросил Чагатаев.

"Не от голода, — ответила Айдым." "У меня от чувства . . . Назар, отчего я чужая?"

"Кому ты чужая, Айдым?" спросил Чагатаев.

"Народ жил с нами, а теперь весь раскочевался," сказала Айдым. — "Ты тоже скоро уйдешь, кто тогда меня помнить будет?"] (213)

When they arrive in civilization, Aidym is no longer hungry, but she suffers from a different pain: the feeling of strangeness or estrangement. She is strange now because the people have dispersed and settled down in different places ("raskochevalsia"). She no longer lives with her people and fears that no one will remember her, that she will be a stranger to everyone. In the Russian original, she asks Chagataev "otchego ia chuzhaia?" which is translated as "why doesn't anyone need me?" but literally means "why am I strange/foreign?" Chagataev assures her that he will remember her and take her with him to Moscow, but when he does so, they become strangers to each other nevertheless. Thus, the physical pain of starvation is contrasted to the pain of the lonely soul. And through Chagataev's consciousness, Platonov expresses the view that we need the other in order to feel our own life and souls:

No nation, not even the Dzhan, can live life split up and scattered. People receive nourishment from one another not only through the bread they eat but also through the soul; through sensing and imagining one another; otherwise, what can they think about, where can they spend the tender, trusting strength of life, where can they scatter their sorrow and find comfort, where can they die an unnoted death? With only the imagination of his own self to nourish him, a man soon consumes his soul, exhausting himself in the worst of poverties and dying in mindless gloom. (130)

[Никакой народ, даже джан, не может жить врозь: люди питаются друг от друга не только хлебом, но и душой, чувствуя и воображая один другого; иначе, что им думать, где истратить нежную, доверчивую силу жизни, где узнать рассеяние своей грусти и утешиться, где незаметно умереть . . . Питаясь лишь воображением самого себя, всякий человек скоро поедает свою душу, истощается в худшей бедности и погибает в безумном унынии.] (221)

The Dzhan nation perishes because, dispersed or "apart," it cannot survive—not because it can no longer be the bearer of a culture, but because it loses the minimal element from which culture can grow: the sense and experience of the other as the self. Here we find the utmost expression of Platonov's original communism, a communism that lies at the origin of the experience of life: where what is in common is the self of the "shared meaning of life." This is the germ of his other revolution, which is a different consciousness of what it means to be in the world, namely the insight that without the other, man cannot feel anything but despair and estrangement. We need the other because we nourish ourselves from the other as a soul, or rather, from the way in which the other is the soul, or dear little life. Life is sustained by the care and imagination of the other because it is in being in another that it can survive.

Thus the material poverty of the Dzhan is contrasted to the spiritual poverty of modern man, and the lack of "spiritual food" as the lack of the other appears as another hell that is perhaps even worse than the famine afflicting the Dzhan. At the end of the novel Chagataev meets another people who also call themselves Dzhan:

> We're Dzhan, replied the old man, and it emerged from his words that every little tribe, every family and chance group of gradually dying people living in the empty places of the desert, the Amu-Darya and the Ust-Yurt, called themselves by the same name: Dzhan. It was their shared name, given to them long ago by the rich beys, because Dzhan means soul and these poor, dying men had nothing they could call their own but their souls, that is, the ability to feel and suffer. The word, *dzhan*, therefore, was a gibe, a joke made by the rich at the expense of the poor. The beys thought that the soul meant only despair, but in the end it was their *dzhan* that was the end of them; they had too little *dzhan* of their own, too little capacity to feel, suffer, think and struggle. They had too little of the wealth of the poor. (141)

> [Мы — джан, — ответил старик, и по его словам оказалось, что все мелкие племена, семейства и просто группы постепенно умирающих людей, живущие в нелюдимых местах пустыни, Амударьи и Усть-Урта, называют себя одинаково — джан. Это их общее прозвище, данное им когда-то богатыми баями, потому что джан есть душа, а у погибающих бедняков ничего нет, кроме души, то есть способности чувствовать и мучиться. Следовательно, слово "джан" означает насмешку богатых над бедными. Баи думали, что душа лишь отчаяние, но сами они от джана и погибли, — своего джана, своей способности чувствовать, мучиться, мыслить и бороться у них было мало, это — богатство бедных.] (230)

Platonov reverses the relationship between poverty and wealth by insisting that in richness there is a different kind of privation due to a lack of being with the other, a lack of the other in the self. Thus, he also inverts the modern myth of salvation through civilization by transforming it into a story about the loss of the "soul." Civilization promises fullness and abundance and insists on a hierarchy of forms of material life, but it loses sensitivity to the life that the other lives in us and the life we live in others. Chagataev has entered the otherworld of the interiority of his self and experienced the life of the other in him, but he is unable to take this experience with him. He cannot carry this world in him as a conscious experience. What he has is only the insight with which the novel ends, for now he knows that he is dependent on others: "Chagataev knew for sure that help could come to him only from another human being" (146).

In this treatment of the myth of the salvational task of modern civilization, Platonov poses a fundamental question about whether communality can persist in the modern world of abundance. If in earlier works, such as *The Foundation Pit* and *Chevengur,* he had shown how the revolutionary historical scheme alienates people from their inner experience of both the past and the present, in *Dzhan* he has definitely discovered how to inquire about the present of the past in terms of inner life or interiority. In this novel he develops a highly specific way of writing about interiority, the soul, the self, and viewing the innermost own of memory as the place of communality. Interiority is often thought of as the ultimate own, the ultimate self. Following Hegel's concept of the negativity of the subject or the personal superego, George Bataille (1988) describes interiority or "Inner experience" as a place of sensitive ecstasy, where the I, the subject, is able to meet and fathom the entire world in himself as a place of fusion of subject and object. Hegel defines interiority as "the wealth of an infinite number of representations, of images," and for him as for Bataille, interiority is understood in Romantic categories as the night of the world, to be attained only through forms of utter negativity, the latter emphasizing an extreme sacrifice of the conscious self (Bataille 1990). It is very interesting to compare and contrast Platonov's concept of inner life with the ideas of these thinkers. Like them, he regards the Inner, or interiority, in terms of a negativity with regard to the conscious self, and he similarly finds in it an infinite number of representations and images. Platonov, however, thinks of these representations as memories, which is to say, the presence of the other, or rather the presence of past meetings in the self. The Inner is not the autonomous space of fusion and a superconscious self that embraces and communicates with the world in itself through desire. At the most, the self in the works of Platonov is the eunuch, the disinterested spectator of people entering and exiting inner life. The Inner, therefore, is where the world in its outer strangeness keeps on living as the own and as the source of communality. The material of the Inner is the afterlife of others in us as the stuff that memories and "dreams are made of."

Moreover, for Platonov the negativity of this realm of experience is not a total negativity per se; it does not belong to a radical transcendence but is an experience that can be had in close proximity to being. This attainment of the experience is viewed not as a radical transgression, but rather through what Heidegger would call *Versunkenheit*—the praxis of falling into the self—because the self is a constantly present other world: the other world of past and present meetings living within us. In a parallel to Rilke's statement that for the elderly the difference between life and death is not so great, Platonov sees extreme poverty as an experience in which the material of the self can be felt as the beginning of an inner world—a world where the difference between the self and the other is not so great.

Thus, Platonov develops the notion of *dzhan*, or soul, as a communal ontology that is to be understood not according to Christian duality in the sense of an immaterial entity opposed to the body, but as access to the common world in the self and as the inner self. What the soul according to Platonov *is*, therefore, cannot really be expressed or experienced consciously. It is the coincidence of the being in which we live and the being which exists in us; it is the communality that we are and from which we constantly move away. *Dzhan* can therefore also be read as a barely concretized literary image of the revolutionary utopia of being at home in the common world, because it is the image of the experience of the world as the self, or the image of the felt presence of others in the interiority of the self.

NOTES

1. Here we see a narrative illustration of entropy, that is, the loss of energy within a system, which Seifrid regards as central to Platonov's writings.

2. "But Chagataev was like a sick man to whom nothing brings pleasure or interest" (Platonov and Chandler, et al. 2007, 9). All further references to this edition are by page number only.

3. The word "narod" in Russian can be translated as both people and nation. In the novel, Dzhan stands for a nation as well as a people.

4. See Kaminskij (2013, 261), who reads *Dzhan* according to the myth of Hermes; Turbin (1965) as a mystery play; Bodin (1991) against the background of biblical legends and the myth of Ahriman; Ingdahl (2000) as gnostic; Zhunturova-Fisherman (2000) as Zoroastrian; and Ismailov (2001) as Sufi.

5. The translation here is slightly incorrect. The food does not "remain," but lingers; dwells in him.

SIX

"The River Potudan"

Love in Existential Poverty

In "The River Potudan" (1937) and the collection of stories that bears its name, Platonov turns his attention to quandaries of marital love in Soviet society from the Revolution onwards. These stories have for different reasons been regarded as marking a shift in interest from "the Great Family of Soviet society to the small natural family" (Günther 2005, 305); that is, a transition from a utopian to a postutopian period, and also as a farewell to asceticism and idealization to a postideological stage.[1] Although there is a turn to the nuclear family and a confirmation of bodily desire, I will argue that it does not signal a change in Platonov's attitude toward official ideology and utopia, but instead is indicative of a modification of his other revolutionary quest for the meaning of existence in common. The treatment of love in "The River Potudan" continues the series of Platonov's works dealing with the sphere of intimate relations. In both *Happy Moscow* and *Dzhan* the relationship with the Great Family of Soviet society is more apparent, since the focus is on revolutionary "free" love in terms of desire, ephemeral meetings, and casual coincidences. Here Platonov moves away from his scrutiny of what we commonly understand to be the avant-garde "communist" flaunting of bourgeois norms of conjugal intimacy as expressed by Aleksandra Kollontai, for instance, who famously stated that satisfying sexual desires should be as simple as drinking a glass of water. In this short story we meet two lovers who know only each other as they embark on the road to marital life. Here he approaches another vision of a revolutionary or proletarian love nurtured by the memory and shared existence of two people who have nothing but each other. And for the first time, Platonov offers us an image of the difficult path of two lovers who ultimately are able to fath-

107

om the opposition between intimate desire and the experience of the other in the Inner of the self.

Set in the first period of stability after the civil war, "The River Potu-dan" tells the love story of Nikita Firsov, a demobilized Red Army sol-dier, and Lyubov Kuznetsova, a medical student. Both think of them-selves as faithful to the Revolution, and neither has any earthly posses-sions or sense of belonging. The story takes place in a postrevolutionary society in which Nikita and Lyubov's (also known as Lyuba) love is both grounded in and inhibited by their memories of the past and their under-standing of the Revolution. Nikita is set on giving and self-sacrifice, and he immerses himself completely in his feelings of love for Lyuba as the wonders of the kinship with another life. Once they are happily married, however, he is unable to consummate it.[2] The demands of a bodily union are different from those of his love for her in terms of the "hidden life of the other," and in their cruelty they become insurmountable for him. It is only through reaching the "beyond of giving"—as *Po-tu-dan'* in the title of the story can be analyzed (more on this below)—in an utter rejection of the self, bordering on death, that Firsov is able to accept the necessity of "taking" the other into his soul, as Platonov puts it. The confirmation of the necessity of consuming their love should not be interpreted in strict terms as a disavowal of Platonov's early critique of a culture based on the passion of the sexes, because the story allows Platonov to thematize the problem of different and conflicting intimate experiences of the other in the self. As the story ends with their bodily union, we have followed a love story that develops primarily in relation to the inner need of the other in the self, and not in relation to desire. Moreover, what Nikita attains in the experience of union with Lyubov is the wish of the heart to share its blood.

A NEW MEMORY

The very first scene introduces the theme of memory and the hope of finding a new meaning to the world. The story begins in a sweeping movement portraying the homecoming of soldiers from the civil war in 1921. It is a period that views itself as a new beginning, a break with both the war and the prerevolutionary past. Because the memory of the past before the Revolution lives on in the revolutionary present, however, the characters are presented as at once new and old. Both nature and the soldiers are returning to life after having been the stage and the actors of war. They are walking on the "trodden-down tracks" (Platonov and Chandler, et. al. 2007)[3] of the conflict, where the grass is growing again. With "faint, astonished hearts," they are coming back to "live as if for the first time" to their "own life and life in general" (ibid.), which can also be translated as their "own and common life" ("k svoei i obshchei zhizni") (426):

> Their souls had changed in the torment of war, during illness and in the happiness of victory, and they were on their way to live as if for the first time, dimly remembering themselves as they had been three or four years ago, for they had turned into quite different people—they had grown up because they were older and they had become more intelligent and more patient and had started to feel inside them the great universal hope which had become the idea of their lives—lives that were small as yet and which had no clear aim or purpose before the war. (213)

> [— они шли теперь жить точно впервые, смутно помня себя, какими они были три-четыре года назад, потому что они превратились совсем в других людей — они выросли от возраста и поумнели, они стали терпеливей и почувствовали внутри себя великую всемирную надежду, которая сейчас стала идеей их пока еще небольшой жизни, не имевшей ясной цели и назначения до гражданской войны.] (Platonov 2010a, 425)

Thus, the beginning establishes a universal perspective within the particular little life that will be the focus of the story. Harboring "the great universal hope" of Communism, the soldiers return with a new awareness of life to the "small lives" that had no aim or meaning before they left. The word for small "nebolshoi" is marked, and in its negation meaning "not big" or "not great," it announces not so much the quality of smallness or mediocrity in their lives as the previous lack of the greatness that they now are apprehending after the Revolution. Yet it is, after all, a return, so what they come back to discover is transformed rather than entirely new. If we contrast Firsov to the universal energy of Moscow Chestnova, it becomes apparent that in his "small life" he embodies the Revolution in an entirely different mode. "The River Potudan" takes place in the 1920s, when the times were arguably still "revolutionary," and yet the focus in this story is on the afterlife and memory of the Revolution. Whereas the lustrous Moscow wished to incorporate and spread "the great universal hope" of the Revolution, Nikita is attempting to carry this hope further in his meager life, because besides his father, he knows and remembers only Lyuba. Nevertheless, as in the case with *Happy Moscow* and several other stories, we will see an opposition between the projection of this "universal hope" onto the future and the experience of it in inner life. It is very significant that Nikita Firsov is a late returner who arrives in autumn when the air is dry and the grass has become "tired of growing" since spring. There is a sense of lateness to the entire story, which will also end in "the cool half dark of late time" (246), something that seems to mark an awareness of the Revolution not as the

breaking of a new dawn but as a sort of silent tragic awareness in the late
time of the memory of this break.

Because Platonov focuses here exclusively on the lives of the destitute
in their singular experience of the change in common existence, his language is much more low-key. The gentle style of the story rhymes well
with the meager resources and needs of the characters. What is done is
done out of necessity, and similarly—what is felt is felt out of necessity.
Caution, goodness, and the lack of a sense of belonging anywhere are
Firsov's distinguishing characteristics. His return is anonymous. He enters his home town in the quiet of the night when all the lights are out
and his father, the only remaining member of his family, is as usual
sleeping "from necessity and because he was tired" (215) ("po neobkhod-
imosti i ot ustalosti"). It is out of necessity that Nikita and Lyuba meet
each other, and it is on the basis of necessity that their love story unfolds.
When Nikita arrives, he remembers Lyuba as well out of necessity, as it
were, for they have no one else. Their first meeting represents a moment
of recognition between two utterly lonely people:

> "Hello!" A woman said to Nikita timidly, from one side.
> This voice immediately touched and warmed him, as if someone
> beloved and lost were answering his call for help. . .
> "You don't remember me?" asked Lyuba.
> "Yes, I do," answered Nikita. "I haven't forgotten you."
> "One should never forget" smiled Lyuba. Her pure eyes filled with
> the mystery of her soul, looked tenderly at Nikita as if admiring him.
> (220)
>
> ["Здравствуйте! — несмело со стороны сказала женщина Никите
> Фирсову.
> И голос тот сразу коснулся и согрел его, будто кто-то, дорогой и
> потерянный, отозвался ему на помощь. . . .
> "Вы меня не помните?" спросила Люба.
> "Нет, я вас не забыл," ответил Никита.
> "Забывать никогда не надо," улыбнулась Люба.
> Ее чистые глаза, наполненные тайною душою, нежно глядели
> на Никиту, словно любовались им.] (431f)

Their memory of each other becomes all the more important due to
their material, social, and existential poverty. After their first meeting,
Lyuba asks Nikita if he will remember her, and he answers that he has no
one else to remember. Not only do they have almost nothing, but they
also remember nothing but each other. Their mutual need is existential in
nature. In the world of the new, the memory of the old will be problematic for them, but it will also be the basis for their belonging to each other.
There is an Oedipal shadow cast over Firsov from prerevolutionary
times, but because it is the necessary basis of their love, it is the shadow
of a memory that somehow competes with the presence of memory itself.
They became acquainted with each other as children, when Nikita's

father wanted to court her mother and ask her to marry him. When he discovered that she was a teacher, however, he stopped visiting her because he felt socially inferior. Firsov similarly views himself as inferior to Lyuba. He is an uneducated carpenter, while she is studying to be a doctor, and the feeling that he has nothing to give renders him temporarily as if crippled and impotent. Although the memory of inferiority will haunt Firsov to the extent that the anticipation of their love becomes unbearable to him, their memory of each other is also the necessary beginning of a love nurtured by the experience of existence in common.

ECONOMIES OF CARE

Firsov and Lyuba's story begins and evolves as the care of the single other in circumstances of extreme poverty. Platonov pays close attention to the details of their everyday life, the so-called *byt*, and how they condition their living and loving. Utterly destitute, Lyuba lives in an economy where each minute, each breadcrumb, and each log is counted. Her only other friend, Zhenya, sometimes brings food and firewood, and she eats so that she will have energy to study and stokes a fire to have light to read. We follow her economy, which is aimed at survival and study, and where Nikita slowly makes a place for himself. At first, however, he contents himself with the little things he can do to help and the few words that Lyuba exchanges with him. After Zhenya dies, Nikita comes to her every day, and they live in a kind of exchange economy:

> As before, Nikita visited Lyuba in her home to help her live and, in return, to receive nourishment for the pleasure of his own heart. (227)

> [Никита по-прежнему ходил к Любе на квартиру, чтобы помогать ей жить и самому в ответ получать питание для наслаждения сердца.] (437)

He constantly gives her whatever he has and attempts to help her in whatever way he can. For instance, he makes a coffin for Zhenya. Lyuba declares that she cannot marry him until she has passed her exams. She is "unable to feel her happiness" until she does so the following spring.[4] In other words, Lyuba invites them to project their love onto the promise of future fulfilment, but Nikita does not have the necessary confidence to wait, and he begins to doubt:

> Nikita heard this distant promise, he was not asking for a greater happiness than that, which, thanks to Lyuba, was already his, and he did not know whether a better happiness even existed, but his heart was chilled from long endurance and from uncertainty: did Lyuba really need someone like him—a man who was poor, uneducated and demobilized. (227)

[Сердце его продрогло от долгого терпения и неуверенности —
нужен ли он *Любе* сам по себе, как бедный, малограмотный,
демобилизованный человек.] (438)

His hesitation concerns the need of the other. He is tormented not
only by his inability to understand what he, in his poverty, can give to
her, but also whether Lyuba really needs him in a higher or more absolute sense. He becomes so weary of his doubts that he falls ill with the flu.
In an act of self-sacrifice, Lyuba takes him home where she can take care
of him. She warms him with her own body, and he is so happy "to sense
more closely someone else's higher, better life and to forget for a while
his own torment" (229) His inability to wait is an aspect of the strength of
his love for and dependence on the other. To further relieve his doubts, as
he recovers he decides to leave town in anticipation of their wedding, but
Lyuba finishes her exams in March and they get married:

> By the evening Nikita Firsov and Lyubov Kuznetsova had registered
> their marriage at the district soviet; they then went into Lyuba's room
> and did not know what to do.
>
> [К вечеру того же дня Никита Фирсов и Любовь Кузнецова
> записались в уездном Совете на брак, затем они пришли в комнату
> Любы и не знали, чем им заняться.] (443)

The contrast between registers in the first and second parts of the sentence—that is, between the high style of the act and the actual experience
of it—reflects perfectly the contrast that appears in their lives. Their common life now seems to be interspersed with a new kind of dignity—they
are married, and we are told that one evening they "had a talk" ("besedo-
vali"). This "beseda" is a conversation about the Revolution and the fact
that it is possible in this new life to have children. It is a talk about
history, which reflects their appropriation of the consciousness of the role
that they have to play in Soviet society. However, the new dignity and
significance of the married couple and their awareness of their historical
role does not help them; on the contrary, it alienates them from their
situation—"they do not know what to do"—and Nikita becomes even
more tormented and powerless as he contemplates the consummation of
their happiness:

> it turned out one had to know how to enjoy pleasure, whereas Nikita
> was unable to torment Lyuba for the sake of his own happiness, and all
> his strength pounded away in his heart, flowing into his throat and
> staying nowhere else. (234)
>
> [Оказывается, надо уметь наслаждаться, а Никита не может мучить
> Любу ради своего счастья, и у него вся сила бьется в сердце,
> приливает к горлу, не оставаясь больше нигде.] (444)

Nikita is ready to sacrifice everything, but consummating their love requires him to give in to the cruel force of his blood. He is unable to

understand his love as the higher need that he feels. She and her life are this "higher," "foreign" secret that remains unattainable for him. He becomes so tormented by his inability to understand their love that he again must seek nonbeing to avoid the torments of his soul and attempt to escape existence itself. They both consider (and Lyuba attempts) suicide, in the belief that that taking (or giving) their lives might satisfy the need to exceed economies of desire, and that only being in different forms of suspension from life will help him.

THE TIME OF THE RIVER AND HIDDEN LIFE

The first place of refuge and suspension is in the eponymous river of the story. In the name of the Potudan River, which runs through Platonov's native Voronoezh district, we hear allusions to the need to understand a hidden life in the reality of facts.[5] The first detail that attracts our attention is the notion of the beyond, the *po tu*, which echoes the expression *po tu storonu* (beyond/on the other side). The flow of the river suggests a different measurement of time and space in which the time of the here and the beyond, finite and infinite, absent and present meet, and what it offers is a beyond to life in its forms of realization. Dal' tells us that the name derives from a folk legend stating that the river was the border up to which the Mongols collected tributes, which is why it is called on the other side of/ beyond tributes" ("po-tu-dan'").[6] Experiencing life and love beyond real tributes and real appearances is also what Firsov is forced to learn, and he will do so with help of the escape that the existential landscape of the river offers him.

The necessary periods in which they suspend their common life are as important in their love story as the evolution of their relationship in accordance with their expectations of its fullness. The frozen river provides them with an existential locus for orienting themselves in these interruptions when they are not able to realize all the promises of their shared future. It offers an image of hidden life, a way in which they can mentally achieve certain forms of nonexistence. They promise to marry when the ice begins to stir, and as they await the consummation of their love, they ask the river about the life it conceals:

> On their days off, Lyuba and Nikita went for walks along wintry paths out of town, or else walked a long way downstream, half embracing, along the ice of the sleeping Potudan'. Nikita would lie on his stomach and look down through the ice to the quietly flowing water. Lyuba settled down next to him and, their bodies touching, they watched the hidden flow of the water and talked of how lucky the Potudan was, because it went all the way to the sea, and this water under the ice would flow past shores of distant lands, where flowers were now growing and singing. After thinking about this for a while, Lyuba

would tell Nikita to get up from the ice at once: Nikita now wore his father's old padded jacket, it was too short and not very warm, and he might catch cold. (230f)

[В дни отдыха Люба и Никита ходили гулять по зимним дорогам за город или шли, полуобнявшись, по льду уснувшей реки Потудани — далеко вниз по летнему течению. Никита ложился животом и смотрел вниз под лед, где видно было, как тихо текла вода. Люба тоже устраивалась рядом с ним, и, касаясь друг друга, они наблюдали укромный поток воды и говорили, насколько счастлива река Потудань, потому что она уходит в море и эта вода подо льдом будет течь мимо берегов далеких стран, в которых сейчас растут цветы и поют птицы. Подумав об этом немного, Люба велела Никите тотчас же вставать со льда; Никита ходил теперь в старом отцовском пиджаке на вате, он ему был короток, грел мало, и Никита мог простудиться.] (441)

The "quietly flowing water" ("ukromnyj potok vody") of the frozen river offers an image of secluded and hidden life that flows beneath the surface. It parallels the time of realization that determines their relationship: the new life that is waiting for them in the form of children and the Revolution and their marriage and the consummation of their love. To Nikita, who decides to be patient and wait, this means that he must mortify or bury his feelings, and although he is frustrated, he finds comfort in the fact that the river is frozen:

And so they were friends, patiently, almost all the long winter, tormented by anticipation of their approaching future happiness. The Potudan river also hid under all the ice all winter, and the winter crops slumbered beneath the snow. Nikita was calmed and even comforted by these processes of nature: it was not only his heart that lay buried until the spring. (231)

[И вот они терпеливо дружили вдвоем почти всю долгую зиму, томимые предчувствием своего близкого будущего счастья. Река Потудань тоже всю зиму таилась подо льдом, и озимые хлеба дремали под снегом, — эти явления природы успокаивали и даже утешали Никиту Фирсова: не одно его сердце лежит в погребении перед весной.] (441)

The fact that it is winter and the river is "buried" under ice until spring is not a coincidence. Death and renewal determine the course of the river as the cyclical year passes and admit of a time frame that is other to their anticipation of future realization. The negative condition in nature confirms and soothes his experience of death or being buried in life. The hidden shared life that they cannot attain makes death appear easier than living.

The final suspension is when Nikita one morning hears Lyuba sobbing and no longer can endure his ambivalence. Tormented by his puritan vision of ideal love and his inability to consummate their marriage, he flees their marital life and goes to live and work at a bazaar, completely denying his identity, feelings, and thoughts. He joins a "beggar" ("nish-chii") headed to a marketplace, where he takes a job as a cleaner, living off the charity of the watchman. He becomes a nobody in order to get rid of his self and forget the love and the tragic moment that he cannot bear: the need to exercise force. Needless to say, his escape is thoroughly nega-tive. He acts very much like a holy fool,[7] not by provocatively misbehav-ing but in the sense of the "rejection of mind" ("otkaz ot uma") typical of negative theology:

> By now his sense of his own self was weak and he thought only those thoughts that wandered into his mind at random. By autumn, most likely, he would have quite forgotten what he was, and, when he saw the world going on around him, would no longer have any idea what it meant; he might then seem to everyone else to be living his life in the world, but in fact he would just happen to be there, existing in uncon-sciousness, in poverty of mind, in absence of feeling, as if in some homely warmth, hiding from mortal grief. (243)

> [Он слабо теперь чувствовал самого себя и думал немного, что лишь нечаянно появлялось в его мысли. К осени, вероятно, он вовсе забудет, что он такое, и, видя вокруг действие мира, — не станет больше иметь о нем представления; пусть всем людям кажется, что этот человек живет себе на свете, а на самом деле он будет только находиться здесь и существовать в беспамятстве, в бедности ума, в бесчувствии, как в домашнем тепле, как в укрытии от смертного горя.] (450)

In this key fragment, Platonov expresses that minimum sense of life on the border of death from which we can begin to get relief from the aporia of our expectations of existence. It is in almost forgetting himself and his being in the world, in "existing in unconsciousness," that Firsov can find comfort. In "poverty of mind" and "absence of feeling" there is a homely warmth that shelters us from tragedy and mortal grief in our inability to live up to the expectations of happiness. Indeed, this "homely warmth" suggests that there is a home in existence on the boundary between life and death, when man is no one with regard to his own self.

THE FORCE OF LATE TIME

It is only after his father happens to come across him that Firsov returns to Lyuba, who has attempted to commit suicide by throwing herself in the river, and they find each other in the consummation of their love. Both have attempted to suspend life in different ways, but now Nikita will return to living with the other in a tragic farewell to his ideal. A key word repeated several times is force or strength ("sila"):

"Lyuba, it's me. I have come."

Lyuba threw the blanket off her face. "Come to me quickly" she begged in her old tender voice, and her arms held out to Nikita.

Lyuba was afraid that all this would suddenly vanish; she seized Nikita by the arms and pulled him to her.

Nikita embraced Lyuba with the force that tries to take the other, the beloved, inside one's yearning soul; but he quickly remembered himself and felt ashamed.

"Not hurting, are you?" asked Nikita.

"No! I'm not," answered Lyuba.

He wanted her, all of her, so she would be comforted, and a cruel pitiful strength came to him. But Nikita's joy from this close love of Lyuba was nothing higher than what he had known ordinarily; he felt only that his own heart now was in command of all his body, sharing its blood with a poor, but necessary creature. (p. 245)

[*"Люба, это я пришел!"* сказал Никита.

Люба откинула одеяло со своего лица. "Иди скорей ко мне!" попросила она своим прежним, нежным голосом и протянула руки Никите.

Люба боялась, что все это сейчас исчезнет; она схватила Никиту за руки и потянула его к себе.

Никита обнял Любу с тою силою, которая пытается вместить другого, любимого человека внутрь своей нуждающейся души; но он скоро опомнился, и ему стало стыдно.

"Тебе не больно?" спросил Никита.

"Нет! Я не чувствую," ответила Люба.

Он пожелал ее всю, чтобы она утешилась, и жестокая, жалкая сила пришла к нему. Однако Никита не узнал от своей близкой любви с Любой более высшей радости, чем знал ее обыкновенно, — он почувствовал лишь, что сердце его теперь господствует во всем его теле и делится своей кровью с бедным, но необходимым наслаждением.] (453f.)

Nikita is able to consummate their love because he approaches her with force. This "cruel, pitiful strength" is such that it "tries to take the other, the beloved, inside one's yearning soul." This is indeed a different experience than the experience of the hidden life of the other as *other* because it is a desire to incorporate the other in the self. If the first love awakes a desire to "give everything necessary," this is a "necessary pleasure" ("neobkhodimoe naslazhdenie") that demands from him that he be the master of his heart because it is sharing its blood with another person. In other words, even at the moment of consummation of desire, Platonov investigates the experience of the other in the self and seeks an ontology of existence in common. At this point, as Platonov emphasizes, Firsov's love has grown—it has become older:

"Will it be all right now, you won't mind living with me?" she asked.

"It'll be all right," answered Nikita. "I've got used to being happy with you now."

"Put more wood on the fire, I'm freezing" said Lyuba.

She was wearing only a threadbare nightdress, and her thin body was chilled to the bone in the cool half dark of late time. (245f)

[Тебе ничего сейчас, не жалко со мной жить? — спросила она.

— Нет, мне ничего, — ответил Никита. — Я уже привык быть счастливым с тобой. — Растопи печку посильней, а то я продрогла, — попросила Люба.

Она была сейчас в одной заношенной ночной рубашке, и похудевшее тело ее озябло в прохладном сумраке позднего времени.] (454)

If life was new and young in the beginning of the story, the time is now late, and their love is old. Nikita has "got used to being happy with her," and the whole story ends in the "the cold half dark of late time" ("v prokhladnom sumrake pozdnego vremeni"). Both these phrases are odd and marked by the experience of alienation in happiness that Platonov has conveyed in the story. Late time should be understood both concretely and metaphorically: the hour is late, it is a late stage in their love, and they are late to realize what the Revolution means as an *afterlife* in the inner self, now that both of them have undergone different forms of death in order to enter the world anew.[8] He sacrifices his ideals and his suffering in order to take her life into his ("vmestit"), to share both in memory and in blood.

Platonov's explorations of intimacy and interiority in "The River Potudan" involve a shift in narrative style from a preoccupation with the great utopian narrative of the Revolution and Soviet modernization to a low-key treatment of the particular existential quandaries of personal life. This shift marks not so much an adjustment in his political approach to Soviet society as it does a changing stance within society toward the early avant-gardism of the revolutionary attitude. In previous stories, Platonov's heroes had in one way or another confronted the grand narrative of the Revolution as a story about achieving the new and had struggled with their marginality as observers, vis-á-vis Soviet society and its forms of alienation. Now, in this later period, the Revolution begins to be thought of as memory, the past, and alienation is treated first and foremost, but not exclusively, as integral to the characters in their relationship with their personal and unique experience in the existential mode of a love story that takes place in existential poverty. However, he also finds new means for describing the discrepancy between the official revolutionary utopia of common being and the other, constantly evasive utopia of existence in common. Platonov describes life and love from the perspective of their entropy, that is, in conditions of existential poverty. Here the characters are extremely exposed to the difficult and conflicting experience of the other—of "foreign life," a "foreign, higher and better life"[9] (chuzhuiu, vysshuiu luchshuiu zhizn') (2010a, 440) as the self and in the self, and yet it is precisely they who attain it.

NOTES

1. As several scholars have remarked, there is an issue of desire related to the Revolution in Platonov's works. Geller (1982, 27) argues that the writer's oeuvre pivots around the evolution of his ideas of love and women, and Philip Ross Bullock (2005) dedicates an entire monograph to the development of his ideas of the feminine. The movement as these and other scholars have described it is from asceticism in his youth to a confirmation of sexual desire in his more mature works. However, it is possible to elaborate further on the nature and history of this affirmation, because the confirmation of bodily desire can be seen as based on the same ideology as the idea he held to in his youth, namely the quest for shared existence.

2. As Eric Naiman (1997, 292) emphasizes, Firsov was a pseudonym that Platonov took in a debate on asceticism when he urged his communist comrades to "donate everything necessary."

3. References below to this edition are by page number only.

4. See also Kornienko (2003, 580), who argues that the story is about the dichotomy of conscious and unconscious life, where the unconscious is to be preferred. The problem, however, is not how to become unconscious, but how to attain the experience of common life in the self.

5. Cf. Lysov (2003).

6. Потудань: р. Воронежской губ., правый приток р. Дона. Берет начало в Нижнедевицком у., где образуется из слияния нескольких мелких речек и протекает по-этому и по соседнему Коротоякскому у., в пределах которого впадает в Дон. 100-верстное течение ее тихое, по илистому дну. По народному преданию, до границ этой реки монголы взымали дань, откуда будто и название "поту-дань." [*Potudan'*: river in Voronezh Guberniia, right-bank tributary to the Don. Originates in the Nizhnedevitsii Uezd, where it is formed by the convergence of several small streams and flows through this and the neighboring Korotoiakskii Uezd, where it empties into the Don. Calm and with a muddy bottom, it is 100 versts (kilometers) long. According to a folk legend, the Mongols collected tributes up to the boundary of this river, whence the name "potu-dan.'"]

7. Several scholars have discussed the theme of holy foolishness in Platonov's works. See, for instance, Thomas Seifrid (1992) and Hans Günther (2012).

8. As Piskunova (2003, 394) notes, this late time can also be related to the late time of the river and a return to life that flows just like the river.

9. This passage is translated in (Platonov and Chandler, et. al. 2000, 228) as "someone else's higher, better life." I use the word "foreign" simply for the clarity of the argument.

SEVEN

The Ecstasy of War

"Inspired People" and "The Return"

This chapter is a reading of two very different short stories: "Inspired People" ("Odukhotvoryennye liudi") (1942) and "The Return" ("Sem'ia Ivanov / Vozvrashchenie") (1946), written during and after World War II. The first story, "Inspired People," is a heroic narrative eulogizing five sailors who died repulsing a battalion of German tanks at the famous November 1941 battle for the village of Duvankoi near Sevastopol. A war correspondent at the time he wrote the story, Platonov was allowed to publish again after several years of silence. The work was well received by other Soviet writers, one reason being that it enhanced the grand narrative of Soviet official propaganda praising the enormous heroic sacrifices of the Soviet troops. By contrast, the second story, "The Return," is critical of glorification of the soldiers as they come home from the war. The father of the family, Aleksey Ivanov, returns filled with the inebriating spirit of victory and is therefore reluctant to face the humble conditions under which his family has been living. The intimate and existential tone of the story shows the main character to be a prisoner of his own ideas about himself and the world. It was widely criticized and failed to reach publication.

Again, we have to do with two stories that deal, albeit very differently, with the great narrative of the history of Soviet society. It is interesting to bring them together, because in both of them, Platonov explores the idea of the Revolution as a form of ecstasy that takes the characters out of themselves. Whereas in "Inspired People," this ecstasy involves oblivion of the inner self as a realm of reflection, questioning, and memory[1] that is positive because it opens the characters to the world, the postwar victory fervor in "The Return" alienates the main protagonist by increasing his sense of self-realization rather than his sensitivity to how others speak in him. There is, of course, a difference between Platonov's attitude at the beginning of the war, when he, like everyone else, was affected by a rise in patriotic sentiment, and his feelings once it was over, when he again probes the experience of being in the midst of the historical moment, but the contrasting treatment of official propaganda in these stories does not primarily reflect a shift in his view of the war itself. What they instead illustrate are two ideas of the Revolution that are not entirely contradictory but chafe against each other in the attempt to make them converge. On the one hand, in "Inspired People," the Revolution is viewed much in accordance with official propaganda, in particular, the heroes' ability to sacrifice themselves for the common cause in a state of complete self-oblivion. On the other hand, the problem in "The Return" concerns coming home after the war not only to the family but also to the own and the self, and in recognizing in the own the presence of a communality that has become other. Here we see how Platonov embraces two ideas of the Revolution that are opposed to each other when they are implemented in real life, in that one insists on oblivion of the Inner and the other on the importance of retrieving the presence of the other in the Inner. These two ideas meet on the ideological level, however, because they both insist on replacing the experience of the self with the experience of common, shared meaning. Both stories tell us about the power of nonbeing in the experience of communality and the potential blindness to the world in a consciousness intent upon realizing an individual path. In "Inspired People," Platonov seems to find a realization of the idea of the communality of being in the party line during the war, whereas in "The Return" this idea is forgotten in the official cult of victory and must be retrieved as a memory of the common in the inner self.

"INSPIRED PEOPLE"

"Inspired People" is rather short—some thirty-five pages. At first glance, the sentiment of the story is not so far from the official view of the so called Great Fatherland War at the time it was written. As mentioned above, in many respects, Platonov follows the general line, according to which the war brought out the true revolutionary spirit in the people: their readiness to sacrifice everything and their ecstatic enthusiasm for the collective spirit. Although such ardor was easily exploited, officially, Platonov did not write the story to comply with the party line. On the contrary, the behavior of these five sailors offers him an image of true Soviet Communism in the form of utterly exposed brotherhood.[2] His letters testify to his personal enthusiasm for the Soviet soldiers and their willingness to "sacrifice," or rather, to exhaust their lives in the midst of the tragedy of war. In a letter to his wife dated August 10, 1942 he wrote,

My most important work at the moment: to write about the five sailors from Sevastopol. Do you remember those who attached grenades to their bodies and threw themselves under the enemy tanks? In my view, this is the greatest episode of the war, and I have been assigned to make a work of art that is worthy of the memory of these sailors. I write about them with all the energy of the soul that I have ever had in me. And if it is successful, this work will bring me, if only remotely, closer to the souls of the fallen heroes. It seems to me that in some respects I am succeeding because I am guided by the inspiration of their heroic deed, and sometimes when I work the manuscript is wet from my tears, but these are not tears of weakness . . . I am creating something like a Requiem in prose. [my translation; T. L.]

[Самая важная моя работа сейчас: пишу повесть о пяти моряках севастопольцах. Помнишь — о тех, которые, обвязав себя гранатами, бросились под танки врага. Это, по-моему, самый великий эпизод войны, и мне поручено сделать из него достойное памяти этих моряков произведение. Я пишу о них со всей энергией духа, какая только есть во мне. И это произведение, если оно удастся, самого меня хоть отдаленно приблизит к душам погибших героев. Мне кажется, что мне кое-что удается, потому что мною руководит воодушевление их подвига, и я работаю, обливая иногда слезами рукопись, но это не слезы слабости. . . . У меня получается нечто вроде Реквиема в прозе.] (Platonov 2013)

Because Platonov considered the heroic combat of these five sailors to be one of the greatest moments of the war, he wanted to inscribe their memory in eternity. He first entitled the story "Requiem" and then "Eternal Glory," but we can also see in the letter that "Inspired People" already seemed to be at work in his mind. The word "odukhotvorennye" has Christian connotations and can be translated as "inspired" in the original religious sense of being elevated, vested, or imbued with or transformed into spirit. He returns several times to the words "spirit" and "soul." Platonov was certain that what he wrote was important and that he himself was inspired or exalted ("voodushevlen") by their heroic deeds. He has the "energy of spirit" to write a worthy story, and he thinks himself capable of coming closer to the "souls" of these people. Considering that he was a Marxist—albeit, as we have seen, critical of materialism—what could the word "spirit" mean for him and why was it so significant? The first clue seems to come in a remark by one of the sailors:

We're going to show the enemy what we're made of, what our lives mean, show them we're inspired people, inspired by Lenin [and Stalin; T. L.] and that they, our enemies, are just skins stuffed with fear for the tyrant Hitler! (Platonov and Bean 1972, 241)[3]

[Сегодня мы должны доказать, в чем смысл нашей жизни, сегодня мы покажем врагу, что мы одухотворенные люди, что мы одухотворены Лениным и Сталиным, а враги наши — только пустые шкурки от людей, набитые страхом перед тираном Гитлером!] (Platonov 2010b, 92)

Here the word "inspired" is explained as referring to the spirit of the communist leaders that has aroused the men's heroism. Yet this is not the dominant line of thought in the story. Platonov seeks the meaning of their exalted spirit in the way in which the war makes the people ecstatic in the sense that it brings them out of their selves and their private lives. He interprets the notion of elevation and spirit as the revolutionary readiness of the dispossessed to sacrifice themselves for shared life on the border between life and death in the extreme conditions of war:

A new strength filled their bodies and he felt capable of great things, and they understood that they had not been born into the world to squander and destroy their lives in fruitless enjoyment of it, but to return it to justice, to their land and people, to give back more than they had received at birth so that human existence might acquire more meaning. (254)

[Тело их наполнилось силой, они почувствовали себя способными к большому труду и они поняли, что родились на свет не для того, чтобы истратить, уничтожить свою жизнь в пустом наслаждении ею, но для того, чтобы отдать ее обратно правде, земле и народу, — отдать больше, чем они получили от рождения, чтобы увеличился смысл существования людей.] (102)

Although Platonov does not explicitly make the connection, he gives us to understand that it was only the Leninist and Stalinist preparation for total war that made possible the experience of war as something sublime, elevated, or lofty ("vysokoe"), as "the greatest, most unknown and most terrible in life" ("samoe velikoe, neizvestnoe i strashnoe v zhizni"). It is significant that instead of the word "sacrifice" to describe what they did, he uses "istratit'," (to waste or exhaust) and "unichtozhit'" (eliminate, destroy). It is their communist background that makes the sailors willing to exhaust life and be reduced to nothing. The people will fight as long as they have a single limb left intact (253). They are ready to be nothing, and this is also what prepares them to enter the world of the common to the fullest. In other words, they are not so much sacrificing themselves as abandoning the very idea of a self to sacrifice. And according to Platonov, this is also what makes them superior to the Germans (who in material respects are markedly superior) and will guarantee them victory. The German soldiers are petty, not ready to "do battle with these all-powerful men who blow themselves up in order to destroy their enemy." (261-63) ("so vsemogushchimi liud'mi, vzryvaiushchimi samykh sebia") (108). Odintsov asserts that "right is on our side" (229) ("Pravda u nas") because they have read Lenin and, therefore, have a suffering soul ready to embrace the world completely.

THE MEANING OF WAR

In "Inspired People," Platonov chooses to portray the deeds of these five sailors from the point of view of victorious Communism as the triumph of forgetfulness of the individual self.

Although the story is in part motivated by love of country, it pivots not so much on patriotism as on the heroes' relationship with death; that is, their patriotic enthusiasm arises from their ability to overcome death in life and achieve immortality. The literary critic A. Chakovskii disapproved of the story, calling it a glorification of death, but as Kornienko (2000) notes, for Platonov it was instead an apotheosis of the immortality of the Soviet soldier. One could add that there is a thanatological aspect to the work, but it is based on an approach to death as the locus of nonbeing, and nonbeing is opposed to the forms of closure of being. In "Inspired People," the war is portrayed as a time when death has become the normal condition of life. The political commissar, Filchenko, observes children playing at death ("igra v smert')" by pretending to bury corpses. This is tragic, and Platonov asks with his heroes how people will be able to go back to life. Yet at the same time the overall condition of death also gives rise to a strange heroic detachment from life.

Although all the characters become lofty heroes, their individual self-oblivion differs. Before the war, most of them were attached to life through memory or hope for the future. The story begins with a sentimental scene of Russian girls singing in a distant village in the Urals. It is echoed later just before the battle as Krasnoselsky remembers his fiancée singing. One character, however, Yura Parshin, is portrayed in marked and significant contrast to the others. Unlike them, he drifts along as a "wide-open and generous source of life" (236). A key to Parshin's character is that he has no concept of himself:

> There was no telling what Yura Parshin had one before the war and before he was enlisted in the navy, for he had a different story for everybody, and never told one person the same story twice. He was not the slightest bit interested in the truth about himself, he was a devotee of fancy, and according to the dictates of his fancy he would tell how he had worked as a lathe operator at a steel works in Leningrad (and he indeed knew how to handle a lathe), or as organizer of entertainment programmes in the Kirov park, or as cook on a merchant ship. (237)

> [Чем занимался Юра Паршин до войны и до призыва во флот, трудно было понять, потому что он говорил всем по-разному и даже одному человеку два раза не повторял одного и того же. Истина о самом себе его не интересовала, его интересовала фантазия, и в зависимости от фантазии он сообщал, что был токарем на Ленинградском металлическом заводе (и он действительно знал токарное дело), либо затейником в Парке культуры имени Кирова, либо коком на торговом корабле.] (90)

What is important in the image of this character is that he is detached from his own person, and as a consequence he is not afraid of death. Death, writes Platonov, has no place in Parshin's being, which is filled with happiness no matter what. His nonchalant attitude is contrasted to that of Filchenko, who has still not come to terms with it:

> But he did not yet know, had not yet learnt, how to encounter death himself, how to die in such a way that death itself would be rendered powerless on meeting him. (238)

> [Но он не знал еще, он не испытал, как нужно встретить и пережить смерть самому, как нужно умереть, чтобы сама смерть обессилела, встретив его.] (91)

How to render death powerless is the central question posed in the story. What happens with almost all soldiers and leads them to a sense of happiness in the midst of combat and death is the realization that the concepts of death and life are unstable. As in Tolstoy's *The Death of Ivan Ilyich*, death is overcome when the difference between the experience of death in life and the life of death is understood. Ordinary peaceful life is a struggle that keeps man enslaved to his needs:

> "It's alright in battle, you don't want anything! But as soon as you're living peacefully, it's one thing after another. You're hungry, or thirsty, or tired, or bored, or . . ."
>
> And Parshin enumerated all the things a man needs when he's living peacefully. Why, he hasn't even got time to live, he's kept so busy satisfying all his needs. And it would seem that only the soldier, when he's in battle, leads a really full and free life, for then he has no need to eat or to drink, but only needs to stay alive, and is content with that happiness alone. (253)

> [Хорошо в бою: ничего не хочешь! А как только мирно живешь, так все время тебе чего-нибудь хочется: то кушать, то пить, то спать, то тебе скучно, то . . .
>
> И Паршин подробно перечислил, что требуется мирно живущему человеку; такому человеку и жить некогда, потому что ему постоянно надо удовлетворять свои потребности. А живет, оказывается, счастливой и свободной жизнью лишь боец, когда он находится в смертном сражении, — тогда ему не надо ни пить, ни есть, а надо лишь быть живым, и с него достаточно этого одного счастья.] (100f)

Platonov captures a strange and paradoxical necessity of life in the ultimate power of death in war. The soldier needs only one thing—"to be alive"—and the reason, at least in this story, is that he must kill as much as possible before he dies himself. Platonov portrays this happiness of war as a fact, without moralizing. Instead, he turns the tragedy of death and dying on its head by pointing to the tragic homelessness or lifelessness of man, who is a prisoner of his needs in peacetime. The "inspired" heroes of Platonov's story are prisoners of war captured in deadly combat, yet they are liberated from the death of life. One after the other they proclaim that they already know death and are ready to die. Parshin exclaims, "There's nothing to worry about. I've seen death and got used to it!" (258) ("Ne strashno, ia videl smert', ia privyk k nei!") (105), and Filchenko echoes him even more strongly: "Let's go out there and die! No life's better than death just now" (259) ("Poshli na smert'! Luchshe ee teper' net zhizni!" (106). At the moment of his death, Filchenko says that his "life's simple destiny" comes so easily to his soul, "which agreed to die and demanded death as much as though it were life" (261). The heroism and spirit of the characters are thus measured against their readiness to accept death as life. It is highly significant that Tsibulko, who survives for a time and is picked up by his squadron after the battle, talks his way into death without sensing any difference. The story ends with the words "he fell silent and died" (263) ("umolk i umer") (109).

For these heroes, death has replaced life as the focus of life, relieving them of their lifeless forms of being and filling them with inspiration. Indeed, it is as if war brings out the true communist potential or spirit in these people. Conversely, in this story Platonov envisions the genuine communist revolutionary spirit as the self-oblivion demanded in combat. There and in the Revolution as well, people are able to abandon their attachment to their personal lives in favor of common, shared existence.

"THE RETURN"

The great postwar story, "The Return" (1946), also entitled "The Ivanov Family," stands in sharp contrast to the heroism of "Inspired People." Here Platonov opposes the officially propagated joyous victory and images of the returning soldiers' heroism to the quiet valor and suffering of those on the home front who fought other sorts of battles. Because it was critical of the party line, the story was in its turn widely criticized by representatives of the literary establishment. The plot revolves around Aleksei Ivanov, a soldier who returns to his wife and two children only to find that he is not at home in a world that has changed since he left. Now his heroism, or rather, his cultivation of the official memory of it, only hinders his understanding of the situation of the family to which he returns.[4] He comes home to discover that in his absence, he was not the only man in his home; besides other men who have helped and also to a certain extent courted his wife, his son has taken over his role as father. Ivanov's new position in his old home does not fit his heroic self-understanding, which is formed by his experience as a soldier, and the "happiness" of victory. The notion of happiness is bracketed here because Platonov views it as a blind spot, while returning also offer a form of grief.

Platonov turns his attention to Ivanov's difficulties in coming back to a world which was his own but has become alien to him in his absence. His family survived without him, yet they continue to need him immensely. His homecoming demands an entirely different return—to an awareness of this need. The story opens with Ivanov in a railroad station waiting for a delayed train. On the third day, after having celebrated the victory and taken farewell from other soldiers for the second time, he meets Masha, a young woman with whom he has a brief affair. The dalliance causes a delay in his journey home and is contrasted to his family, who go to the village station every day to see if he has finally arrived. He and Masha feel "orphaned without the war," because it offered them a meaning to their existence—a kind of home and a sense of belonging. Masha feels that she seems to be living in a foreign land ("na chuzhbine"). Their relationship gives them some final comfort and distraction before returning to the real homes that have also become alien to them:

> Ivanov and Masha felt orphaned now without the army, but Ivanov could never stay sad or despondent for long; if he did, he would feel as if someone were laughing at him from a distance and being happy instead of him, while all he did was scowl like a half-wit. (Platonov and Chandler, et. al, 2008, 283)[5]

> [Иванов и Маша чувствовали себя сейчас осиротевшими без армии; однако Иванов не мог долго пребывать в уныло-печальном состоянии; ему казалось, что в такие минуты кто-то издали смеется над ним и бывает счастливым вместо него, а он остается лишь нахмуренным простачком.] (417)

The euphoria of war had become the ordinary condition of life, and now it has been replaced by the ecstasy of victory. This ecstasy, however, is a form of being outside of the self, not in a world of common, shared meaning. The fact that "Ivanov could never stay sad or despondent for long" is not because he is constantly happy, but because there is always someone there to be "happy instead of him." Happiness is the general mood of the times, but as Platonov shows us, this atmosphere neglects what life really demands. Estrangement in life outside of war pursues him all the way to his home, which he senses is "strange and rather hard to understand" (291) ("Stranen i eshche ne poniaten byl Ivanovu rodnoi dom") (424).

In sharp contrast to his own ecstatic fervor, Aleksei Ivanov arrives to find that his family has lived under very harsh conditions and that his children have been forced to behave as grown-ups. The difference in their respective lives comes between them, and Aleksei learns that a widower by the name of Semen Evseevich has been there to look after his children and has made a few intimate approaches to his wife. At night, when the children are asleep, he begins to interrogate his wife about the men that she has met and how she has lived, and she tells him sincerely about the hardships of her lonely life with a job and two children. His questions about concrete facts appear false and insincere in the light of his own lies and indifference toward the family. Indeed, what Platonov slowly brings to our attention is Ivanov's utter lack of empathy and sense of communion with his family. As is highlighted by the constant use of the Russian word "rodnoi," meaning "kindred, close," he wants to return to homeliness and kinship. Yet Ivanov's longing appears all the more quaint in that he senses the strangeness of the history that has come between him and his family.

As it turns out, his "return" only serves to increase his estrangement from the world, and he decides to leave his family and go back to Masha, with whom he can share at least the experience of being homeless. In the morning he boards a train, but then he sees his children running after it, begging him to come back. This is the climax of the story—the sublime moment that gives him an insight into real life and the tragedy of his self-understanding and self-interest:

> Ivanov closed his eyes, not wanting to see and feel the pain of the exhausted children now lying on the ground, and then felt a kind of heat in his chest, as if the heart imprisoned and pining within him had been beating long and in vain all his life and had only now beaten its way to freedom, filling his entire being with warmth and awe. He suddenly recognized everything he had ever known before, but much more precisely and more truthfully. Previously, he had sensed the life of others through a barrier of pride and self-interest, but now, all of a sudden, he had touched another life with his naked heart. (308)

> [Иванов закрыл глаза, не желая видеть и чувствовать боли упавших обессилевших детей, и сам почувствовал, как жарко у него стало в груди, будто сердце, заключенное и томившееся в нем, билось долго и напрасно всю его жизнь и лишь теперь оно пробилось на свободу, заполнив все его существо теплом и содроганием. Он узнал вдруг все, что знал прежде, гораздо точнее и действительней. Прежде он чувствовал другую жизнь через преграду самолюбия и собственного интереса, а теперь внезапно коснулся ее обнажившимся сердцем.] (439)

At first Aleksei tries to ignore his poor children running after him and pleading with him to return. However, it is as if his "naked" heart is stronger than he is, and he cannot keep it from beating at this horrible sight. His heart breaks through the "limits of his love for himself and his own interests" so that he finally can feel its barrenness. "The Return," Platonov tells us, is a story not about victory but about the struggle of turning from one ecstatic mode of being in the world to the ecstasy of experiencing the other in the self. It is only through the realization of this conflict that Ivanov discovers his capacity to feel and sense his family. He gets off the train because through his alienation he has discovered the others who are his own, his children in himself. Thus, Platonov criticizes the official postwar propaganda because he sees the ecstasy of war lingering on in the form of self-infatuation, which is also a forgetfulness of being with others in the world and in the self.

In these two war stories, Platonov shows us different ecstatic modes of being during and after the war, but he does not oppose them to any truer or more authentic form of existence. He does not portray the lack of self in the ecstatic moment of being in the world as problematic. On the contrary, what he tells us is that being in the common world implies a loss of self. What the contrast between these two stories shows us instead are different ways in which the self is abandoned in favor of communality—one corresponding and one opposed to the party line at the time. In "Inspired People," the ecstasy of war is linked to devotion to nonbeing, to existence on the border of life and death where individuality is extinguished, which is precisely what the situation of war demands. In the case of "The Return," Platonov shows us that the joyous ecstasy of victory leads to a neglect of what postwar existence really demands. Thus, in another revolutionary recognition of the meaning of common existence, Aleksei Ivanov is forced to realize that the life of others pulsates in himself and his own naked heart.

NOTES

1. Cf. Bataille (1988, 3), who defines the Inner experience as follows: "Inner experience responds to the necessity in which I find myself—human existence with me—of challenging everything (of putting everything into question) without permissible rest."

2. See also Geller (1982, 393), who writes that the war becomes the "common task" ("obshchee delo") about which the writer has always dreamt.

3. References below to this edition are by page number only. Stalin's name was excised from the edition on which this translation was based.

4. Angela Livingstone (2000, 115) makes an interesting comparison between Ivanov's return and that of Ulysses, arguing that the war and home are presented as two entirely different and in some ways opposed spheres.

5. References below to this edition are by page number only.

Afterword

The Memory of Utopia and the Utopia of Memory

The fall of the Soviet Empire in 1991 resulted in an avalanche of "memory" recordings and "memory studies." There was a call to "recover memory" in Eastern Europe to fill the lacunae in the history of personal experiences left after the repressions and censorship that had become a permanent part of Soviet culture. This collection of accounts of Soviet reality has been interpreted in terms of a "collective memory" or "cultural memory" that needed to be retrieved from the imposed historical narrative of the Soviet Union. This notion, however, has much in common with the writing of a new historical narrative in an uncensored form.[1] At the core of the politics around the "memory" of the 1917 Revolution, which indeed also concerns the historical narrative of the event, lies the fundamental question, "What *was* the Bolshevik Revolution?" This issue, of course, divides into subquestions such as whether the upheaval can be understood as a revolution, the extent to which it was socialist, and if it was, whether it survived the Bolshevik abuse of power as a socialist revolution. These questions are certainly problematic politically, not least because despite the obvious atrocities committed by the communist regime, leftists have not entirely abandoned the claims of Marxists and revolutionaries that they are not only telling a different historical narrative from a different perspective, but that the Revolution launched Russia onto a unique historical path.

Marxists seek to challenge the hegemonic ideas of society and reality inherent in capitalist societies by arguing that these concepts are merely expressions of ideology. Yet already, Lenin made ideology and idealism officially recognized essential features of Soviet policy and culture, so that, as Bertholt Brecht allegedly said to Walter Benjamin (2007, 97) in 1938,[2] in the Communism of Soviet Russia the struggle with ideology simply became a new ideology. Nevertheless, the question that has come up especially in Marxist studies of communist societies after the fall of the Berlin Wall is whether, despite the apparent flaws of state Communism, the 1917 Revolution and Soviet culture offered a perspective on history that is somehow different from the hegemonic viewpoint of the capitalist West.

The legacy or memory of the Revolution is of course linked to the question of how Communism, its literature, and its legacy should be understood today. In *The Seeds of Time,* Fredric Jameson reads Platonov's *Chevengur* through precisely this prism. From a different angle, in *The Inoperative Community,* Jean-Luc Nancy (1991b) poses a similar question with his notion of literary Communism, asking what can be saved of the idea of Communism after the dark record of its implementation in Russia and Eastern Europe. Is it possible to reach an understanding of Communism in literature that is not communist literature? We are offered a kind of answer to these questions in Platonov's *literary revolution,* which naively reflects and records the grotesque and dismal realization of the Revolution in the experience of its faithful agents. And it does so in a strangely apolitical political way, because Platonov's idea of Communism goes beyond and in many ways contrary to its political realization. Throughout his oeuvre, his account of the most terrifying aspects of Soviet history resists reading it as resistance to Communism, for he insists on a meaning of the ideology that both reveals and is concealed in the October Revolution and its subsequent implementation. Almost all his heroes are faithful to the party and mean well, yet many of them become executioners precisely because of their belief in Communism. This is most notably incarnated in Chepurnyi in *Chevengur.* Through these figures, however, and generally in the way he reveals the disastrous mechanisms at work in the communist interpretation of history as a new transcendent rational logic, he does not simply launch a critique of political utopia. In other words, we cannot agree with those who have argued that Platonov was a "good" Communist throughout his life, a believer, an ideologue clinging to the "good" utopia of the socialist revolution and its promise to emancipate mankind, and yet also perspicacious enough to recognize how the ideals went wrong in their realization. To do so would be to adopt a political position, but Platonov persistently resists taking such a stance. What he instead distinguished and cherished was a facet of the communist utopia that was at work both in the terrifying implementation of Communism and in the dreams of postrevolutionary society, but which was not in accord with the historical narrative of the Revolution. This aspect can be seen as the promise of an understanding of existence that takes into account participation in common being as an experience that is equally or even more fundamental than the experience of the self.

As Platonov sees it, the experience of being in common involves the fact that we ourselves are inhabited by the world, and what is more, that we are nothing but this world. This notion contains a fundamental critique of or opposition to modern subjectivity and its view of individual autonomy as the human essence. Platonov's characters do not think autonomously or detached from reality. Their ruminations are always a response to the incongruities of the world in the form of a sense of longing or a lack of belonging. Failing to keep in step with the general pace and measure of time as Communism is put into practice in Soviet society, the heroes of several works begin to explore a different experience of shared being. Platonov seems to argue that the Revolution reveals that existence is located in between two forms of ecstasies or being in common in the world outside of the self, and that there is no third choice: *tertium non datur*. Real Soviet Communism is presented as the ecstatic appropriation of this quasi-rational historical narrative about the foundation of a community and home for all, which is a sphere outside of the self in the sense that it is oblivious of the past and the world that inhabits the Inner. This is how he interprets the consequence of the well-known promise of Communism to create an ideal society or utopia in real life. What opposes this ecstasy, however, is not subjectivity or a person capable of reflection, but at the most a sensitivity to the different ecstasy of the Inner, which consists in the loss of the conscious, social, or historical self in the barely distinguishable flow of dreams and memories. Somewhere between these temporalities, the self is this sensibility, lost and longing to be at home in the world as it was in dreams—that is, at home in a world that remains alien although it is intimate and remains intimate although it is alien. In other words, the self is thought of as the in-between of two forms of ecstatic existence in common: one is "Outer" and illuminated and working to realize the Revolution and build Soviet society, and the other is the "Inner" and nocturnal experience of the world in the self. These two forms of being in common are incongruous, and although they are not entirely incompatible and correlate with the same political idea, in practice they chafe against each other. One point of divergence has to do with time, and another with the sense of belonging. With regard to the difference in time, Platonov shows that whereas the official revolutionary historical narrative insists on a scheme of historical succession that begins with the Revolution superseding the past and moving on through ever new stages to future happiness, the shared being of inner life is the experience of the simultaneous all-presence in the self of the past, present, and future forms of the world. Further, building the future home for all in society goes wrong not only because it is utopian or because the builders are corrupt but because it does not account for the common Inner of the world and the earth. The sense of belonging to a common existence cannot be projected onto external realizations but must also—except, as "Inspired People" suggests, perhaps in wartime— be grounded in the Inner. Communism is strong in war because it fosters total oblivion of the self as a means of overcoming death. In peacetime, however, it needs the Inner experience of belonging—it needs memory.

Moreover, to the extent that the modern world in general and the realization of Communism in particular prefer the illuminated world of outer appearance, the nocturnal experience of shared existence in the Inner is also diminished or even extinguished. The postrevolutionary world is a world that has "cut short the mystery of time," which is also understood as the "mystery of life." The experience of the Inner, therefore, acquires a memory of what has been forgotten. It is an otherworld, like the distant locus of the darkness in *Happy Moscow* or of the river in "The River Potudan," and can only be attained through an understanding of the impasses of modern existence. Thus, either duped or expelled from the march of history, Platonov's heroes seek in things forgotten or in dreams they are barely able to retrieve another forgotten or lost experience of the world and another experience of meaning. This experience of Inner common being is not revolutionary in the sense of an "idea of a new foundation or a reversal of sovereignty," as Jean-Luc Nancy (1991b, xl) writes, but rather in the inward sense that there is a revolutionary potential in the recognition of "the incessantly present moment at which existence-in-common resists every transcendence that tries to absorb it" (ibid.). As is the case with Platonov, the transcendence to which Nancy contrasts the Revolution can be construed as the transcendence of "outer" time and the "outer" self that often seeks to manifest itself in various forms of possession. It consists in the experience of the common world in the inner self, which always escapes these forms. We can add with Platonov, therefore, that we must recognize that existence-in-common resists any subjectivity that tries to absorb it. He shows us again and again how shared existence lives on in our inner world in a way that cannot be grasped according to the parameters of subjectivity because existence in common consists in being outside of ourselves within ourselves. Platonov's subject is not a person capable of reflection but a spectator, a eunuch that keeps a house inhabited by others as impressions, words, memories—in other words, a guardian of a self-inhabited by the world in himself but unable to communicate with it there.

Because Platonov insists on the ability to experience but inability to communicate with the presence of others in the self, his conception of the communal ecstasy of inner life is distinct from Bataille's and perhaps to a certain extent also Nancy's. These two thinkers differ in their respective understanding of communication, but both of them conceive of the inner self as a place in which it can occur. For Platonov, however, although communication is always at work and the voices of others speak in the Inner self, we cannot communicate with them. If Bataille insists on Inner experience as the realm of fusion, Nancy (1991b, 29) speaks of a sharing, a coappearance and "com-pearance" in dislocation, an exposition of singularities to each other "inasmuch as being-in-common is not a common being."[3] By common being Nancy means something like the communal identity or collective body that is characteristic of totalitarian societies, as Arendt has shown beyond doubt. In Platonov's works, however, being-in-common and common being are confused in both the inner and the outer worlds, perhaps and in particular because common being itself is neither an identity nor an entity or essence. His common being has a body and is incarnated primarily in the proletariat and consequently in the destitute. In other words, there is an ideological factor that transforms the particular into a bearer of the universal. It must be added, however, that this body is a common being not because the proletariat constitutes a transcendent community, but because living as it does without belonging, possessing, or subjectivity, it makes no claim whatever to universality.

Through the Revolution, Platonov also invites us to consider the difficulty of rendering the experience of the people as an experience in its own right. The utterly destitute are beings on the border of the conscious and unconscious, being and nonbeing, and the experience of themselves as the own and as the other. The poor live in closer proximity to unconsciousness, death, nature, and each other. Moreover, he seems to be saying that they are more exposed to the workings of communication and others as the self. It is in their existence that he finds the richness of poverty, because it is there in necessity that the utter exposure of the world is felt. Discrepancies in the experience of time and the time of experience, therefore, become more apparent in the existence of the poor. In other words, one could say that it is because they have no sense of their particularity that they can say something about the universal. Their lack of a home in the outer world enables them to show that dreams and the inner world offer an experience of home.

Platonov's approach to the Revolution both confirms and undoes the Soviet myth of the common being of the proletariat, because from within this myth he finds the means of writing about existence in common . In doing so, he also shows us an alternative to realism and Socialist Realism, or, to use Nancy's term, a "literary communism" that is not identical with communist literature. His realism is not driven by the aspiration to find a narrative representation of social and historical reality coupled through the education of the modern reader to a consciousness of society and its aporias, or, as in the case of socialist realism, to a correct "revolutionary consciousness." He incessantly records the reality of the mishaps and misunderstandings to which the so-called "revolutionary consciousness" leads, and tracks the way in which it points to an experience of reality that is not perfectly real. It is in the misunderstandings, mistakes, and errancy of the poor that Platonov's realism can be found, because it is in them that our relation to the common world can be sensed. The absurdism, folksiness, and fairy-tale-like manner in which he renders the post-revolutionary world serves to capture the "truth of the untruth." The problem with the myth of the Communist utopia, as Platonov tells it, is not the myth itself, but what happens when the myth purports to be real; that is, claims to be truth or logos. The meaning and reality of the in-between of experience begins to emerge not in a better comprehension of reality, but through a mythical awareness. What Platonov ultimately finds in the interior is but the presence of the exterior or the other of the world in the self, and what he finds in the exterior is for the most part the longing of the other and the projection of a world or a self upon itself.

Platonov's utopia, the utopia of the experience of the poor, is a utopia of being *in* existence—and it can be grasped as the happy nonplace of being in common that we are but generally cannot attain in our experience of the world. It has the form of memory, which must be understood not as the memory of the past but as the forgotten memory of a common presence of what constantly evades us. Thus, in retrieving the experience of common being, Platonov also suggests a different understanding of the problem of personal memories during the postrevolutionary implementation of Soviet Communism. He calls for a comprehension of what that existence has become and is constantly becoming that is different from our understanding and projections of the self. In other words, the Revolution can be thought of as the entry to an understanding of a flickering existence in common that is often lost to us in the way that we usually relate to existence. The Revolution, which constantly wanted to present itself as a new foundation, appears in Platonov's works as a nonground, an *Ungrund* on which nothing "new" could be constructed, and yet from which the entire Revolution would emerge. The promise or utopia of the proletarian revolution was to be the beginning of a memory of the significance of the immense presence of the insignificant, meaningless, and alienated world in the self, the significance of insignificant existence in common. Although his writings carry within them memories of the consequences of the revolutionary and political utopia, they were driven by the literary question of retrieving this forgotten and revolutionary utopia of memory.

NOTES

1. See Nora (2002).
2. "Brecht, last night: 'There can't be any doubt about it any longer: the struggle against ideology has turned into a new ideology.'"
3. He goes on: "Finitude compears, that is to say it is exposed: such is the essence of community."

References

Agamben, Giorgio. 1993. *The Coming Community*. Translated by Michael Hardt. Minneapolis: University of Minnesota Press.

Anninskii, L. I. 2014. "Otkrovenie i sokrovenie: Maksim Gorkii i Andrei Platonov." In *Filosofskoe Delo Andreia Platonova*. Voronezh: Izd. dom VGU.

Apelboin, Anne. 2002. "Metaphorical Animals and the Proletariat." *Essays in Poetics*, 27.

Barsht, Konstantin. 2003. "Platonov i Vernadskij: nesluchajnye sovpadenija." In *"Strana Filosofov" Andreja Platonova: Problemy tvorchestva. Vypusk 5*, ed. N. V. Kornienko. Moscow: IMLI RAN, 319–27.

Barthes, Roland. 1953. *Le degré zéro de la Littérature*. Paris: Éditions du Seuil.

———. 1968. "L'Effet de réel." *Communications* 11.

Bataille, Georges. 1929. "L'informe". In Documents No. 1, Paris.

———. 1985. *Visions of Excess. Selected Writings, 1927–1939*. Translated by Allan Stoekl. Minneapolis: University of Minnesota Press.

———. 1988 *Inner Experience*. Translated by Leslie Anne Boldt. Albany: State University of New York Press.

———. 1990. "Hegel, Death and Sacrifice." Translated by Jonathan Strauss. *Yale French Studies, 78*, On Bataille.

———. 1997. *The Bataille Reader*, ed. Fred Botting and Scott Wilson. Oxford: Blackwell Publishers.

Benjamin, Walter. 1994. *The Correspondence of Walter Benjamin, 1910–1940*, ed. Gershom Scholem and Theodor W. Adorno, translated by Manfred and Evelyn Jacobson. Chicago and London: The University of Chicago Press.

———. 1999 "Moscow." In *Selected Writings, Volume 2, 1917–1934*. London and Cambridge, MA: Belknap University Press.

———. 2007. *"Conversations with Brecht."* In *Aesthetics and Politics*. Translated and edited by Ronald Taylor. London: Verso.

Bethea, David M. 1989. *The Shape of Apocalypse in Modern Russian Fiction*. Princeton, NJ: Princeton University Press.

Blanchot, Maurice. 1995. *The Work of Fire*. Stanford, CA: Stanford University Press.

Bocharov, S. G. 1971. "Veshchestvo sushchestvovaniia" in *Problemy khudozhestvennoi formy sotsialisticheskogo realizma*. Vol. 2. Moskva: xx, pp. 310–50.

———. 1985. "Platonov". In *O khudozhestvennykh mirakh*. Moscow: Sovetskaia Rossiia.

Bodin, Per-Arne. 1991. "The Promised Land–Desired and Lost: An Analysis of Andrej Platonov's Short Story 'Dzan.'" *Scando-Slavica, 37*.

Borenstein, Eliot. 2000. *Men without Women: Masculinity and Revolution in Russian Fiction, 1917–1929*. Durham, NC: Duke University Press.

Brodsky, Joseph. 1986. "Catastrophes in the Air" in *Less than One: Selected Essays*. New York: Farrar, Strauss and Giroux.

Chandler, Robert. 2003. "Platonov i Sredniaia Aziia." In *"Strana Filosofov" Andreia Platonova: Problemy Tvorchestva. Vypusk 5*. Moscow: IMLI RAN.

Clark, Katerina. 1981. *The Soviet Novel. History as Ritual*. Chicago and London: The University of Chicago.

Culler, Jonathan. 2007. "The Realism of *Madame Bovary*," *MLN* 122, 4 (September). Online at http://muse.jhu.edu/article/228957. Accessed 20160706.

Dhooge, Ben. 2007. *Tvorcheskoe preobrazovanie iazyka i avtorskaia kontseptualizatsia mira u A. P. Platonova*. Dissertation, Universiteit Gent.

Geller, Mikhail. 1982. *Andrei Platonov v poiskach schastiia*. Paris: Ymca-Press.

Gladkov, Fedor. 1926. *Tsement*. Moscow/Leningrad: Zemlia i Fabrika.

Günther, Hans. 2011. *Po obe storony utopii*, Moscow: NLO.

Hansen-Löwe, Aage. 2012. "Platonov's *Chevengur* between Defamiliarization and Compassion." In *Andrei Platonov. Style. Context. Meaning, Ulbandus. The Slavic Review of Columbia University* vol. 14, pp. 3–36.

Heidegger, Martin. 1996 *Being and Time*. Translated by Joan Stambaugh. Albany: State University of New York Press.

———. 1998. "Letter on Humanism," in *Pathmarks*, edited by William McNeill. Cambridge, UK: Cambridge University Press.

———. 2001 *Sein und Zeit*. 18. Auflage Tübingen: Max Niemayer Verlag.

Hodel, Robert. 2001. *Erlebte Rede bei Andrej Platonov von V zdezdnoj pustyne bis Cevengur* in *Slavische Literaturen, Band 23*. Frankfurt am Main: Peter Lang.

Ingdahl, Kazimira. 2000. "Andrej Platonov's Revolutionary Utopia. A Gnostic Reading." *Wiener Slawistischer Almanach* 46, 17–44.

Ismailov, H. 2001. "'Džan' as a Sufi treatise." In *Essays in Poetics* 26: 72–82.

Jameson, Fredric. 1994. "Utopia, Modernism and Death." In *The Seeds of Time*. New York: Columbia University Press.

Kaminskij, Konstantin. 2013. "Naked Soul on Naked Earth. Economics and Ethnogenesis of Džan." *Die Welt der Slaven* LVIII: 261–75.

Karpov, A. V. 2009. *Russkii Proletkul't. Ideologiia, Estetika, Praktika*. St. Petersburg: Izd. Sankt-Peterburgskogo universiteta profsoiuzov.

Kornienko, Natal'ia. 1999. "Proletarskaia Moskva zhdet svoego khudozhnika," (K tvorcheskoi istorii romana). In *"Strana Filosofov" Andreia Platonova: problemy tvorchestva*. Vypysk 3. Moscow, 1999: 357–71.

———. 2003. "Khudozhestvennaia funktsiia oppozitsii soznatel'noe-nesoznatel'noe v rasskaze 'Reka Potudan.'" In *Strana Filosofov' Andreja Platonova: problem tvorčestva. Vypusk 5. Jubilejnyj*: 579–82.

———. 2005. "Chevengurskie mechtaniia o novom cheloveke v stat'iakh Platonova 1920–x gg." In *"Strana Filosofov" Andreia Platonova: Problemy Tvorchestva*. Moskva: IMLI-RAN, pp. 483–518.

———. 2010. *Nepovskaya Ottepel'. Stanovlenie instituta sovetskoi literaturnoi kritiki*. Moscow: IMLI RAN.

Kostov, Heli. 2000. *Mifopoetika Andreia Platonova v romane Schastlivaia Moskva*. Dissertation, University of Helsinki. Helsinki: Slavica Helsingiensa.

Lane, Tora. 2011. "A Groundless Foundation Pit?" Ulbandus Review, *14* (Andrei Platonov: Style, Context, Meaning): 61–75.

———. 2014. "Giving Away the Giving: Love According to Platonov in 'Reka Potudan.'" In *Med blicken österut: hyllningsskrift till Per-Arne Bodin*, ed. Per Ambrosiani, Elisabeth Löfstrand, Ewa Teodorowicz-Hellman. Skellefteå: Artos & Norma, 2014, Vol. 23, [Stockholm Slavic Papers]: 207–16.

———. 2016. "Platonov's *Chevengur*: Disorientation and the Quest for a Transcendental Home in the World." In Marcia Sa Cavalcante Schuback and Tora Lane, eds. *Dis-Orientation*. Lanham, MD: Rowman and Litttlefield: 173–86.

———. 2017. *Läsningar av Andrej Platonov*. Stockholm: Ersatz.

Lane, Tora and sá Cavalcante Schuback, Marcia, (eds.). 2014. *Dis-Orientations. Philosophy, Literature, and the Lost Grounds of Modernity*. Lanham, MD: Rowman and Littlefield.

Lenin, V. I. 2008 "Rough Draft of a Resolution on Proletarian Culture." In V. I. Lenin, *On Culture and Cultural Revolution*. Rockville, MD: Wildside Press.

Livers, Keith. 2000. "Scatology and Eschatology: The Recovery of the Flesh in Andrei Platonov's *Happy Moscow*." *Slavic Review* 59, 1: 154–82.

Livingstone, Angela. 2002. "Danger and Deliverance. Reading Andrei Platonov." *Slavonic and East European Review* 80, 3: 401–62.

———. 2000. "Motiv vozvrashcheniia v rasskaze Platonova "Vozvrascshenie." In *Tvorchestvo Andreia Platonova. Issledovaniia i materialy*. St. Petersburg: Nauka.

Lukács, Georg. 1971. *The Theory of the Novel. A Historico-philosophical Essay on the Forms of Great Epic Literature.* Translated by Anna Bostock. Cambridge, MA: The MIT Press.

Lysov, Aleksandr. 2003. "'Moi Lugovoi Iordan' . . . Andreia Platonova (O natsional'noi kharakterologii i kul'turnoprirodnykh atributsiakh v rasskaze 'Reka Potudan.'" In *"Strana Filosofov" Andreia Platonova: problemy tvorchestva.* Vypusk 5. Moscow: IMLI RAN: 376–87.

Magun, Artem. 2010. "Otritsatel'naia revoliutsiia Andreia Platonova." http://magazines.russ.ru/nlo/2010/106/ma7.html.

Malygina, N. 2009. "Kommentarii." In Andrei Platonov, *Sobranie sochinenii v 8-kh tomakh:* vol. 2. *Chevengur. Kotlovan.* Moscow: Vremia.

Markstein, Elisabeth. 1978. "Der Stil des Unstils: Andrej Platonov." *Wiener Slawistischer Almanach* 2: 115–39.

Marx, Karl. 1975. *Economic and Philosophical Manuscripts* in *Karl Marx: Early Writings.* Translated by Rodney Livingstone and Gregor Benton. Harmondsworth, UK: Penguin Books.

———. 1976. *Theses on Feuerbach.* Peking: Foreign Language Press.

———. 2005. "Letters from Deutsch-Französische Jahrbücher." In Karl Marx and Friedrich Engels, *Collected Works,* 3: 133–45. New York: International Publishers.

Mayer-Rieckh, Chiara. 2011. *Memory and Wholeness in the Work of Andrei Platonov, Valentin Rasputin and Andrei Tarkovskii.* Dissertation, submitted at the School of Slavonic and East European Studies, University College London.

Meerson, Olga. 1997 and 2000. *Svobodnaia veshch'. Poetika neostraneniia u Andreia Platonova.* [*A Free Thing: The Poetics of Refamiliarization in Andrei Platonov's Work*]. Oakland, CA: Berkeley Slavic Specialties, (republished, Novosibirsk: Russia: Nauka).

———. 2001. "Andrei Platonov's Re-familiarization: The Perils and Potencies of Perceptive Inertia." In *Essays in Poetics,* 26: 21–37.

Mikheev, Mikhail. 2003. *V mir platonova cherez ego iayzk.* Moscow: Izdatel'stvo moskovskogo universiteta MGU/ Im Werden Verlag.

Mørch, Audun J. 1998. *The Novelistic Approach to the Utopian Question. Platonov's Čevengur in the Light of Dostojevskij's Anti-Utopian legacy.* Oslo: Scandinavian University Press.

Naiman, Eric. 1988. "Andrej Platonov and the Inadmissibility of Desire." *Russian Literature,* 23 (4): 319–65.

———. 1997. *Sex in Public. The Incarnation of Early Soviet Ideology.* Princeton, NJ: Princeton University Press.

———. 2014. "Afterword." Slavic Review, 73 (4): 801–4.

Nancy, Jean-Luc. 1991a. "The Unsacrificiable." *Yale French Studies,* No. 79: *Literature and the Ethical Question:* 20–38.

———. 1991b. *The Inoperative Community.* Translated by Peter Connor and Lisa Garbus. Minneapolis: University of Minnesota Press.

———. 2000. *Being Singular Plural.* Translated by Robert Richardson and Anne O'Byrne. Stanford, CA: Stanford University Press.

Nora, Pierre. 2002. "Reasons for the Current Upsurge in Memory." In *Eurozine,* http://www.eurozine.com/articles/2002–04–19-nora-en.html. Accessed September 12, 2016.

Novalis. 2013. *Hymnen an die Nacht.* http://www.gutenberg.org/files/43821/43821-h/43821-h.htm. Accessed September 27, 2016.

Penkina, Natal'ia Viktorovna. 2005. *Filosofskie idei prozy Andreia Platonova.* Dissertation. Nizhnevatorsk.

Petrov, Petr. 2011. "The Industry of Truing: Socialist Realism, Reality, Realization." *Slavic Review,* 70 (4): 873–92.

Piskunova, Anastasiia. 2003. "Na beregu Reki Potudan.'" In *"Strana Filosofov" Andreja Platonova: problem tvor chestva. Vypusk 5. Jubilejnyj.* ed. N. V. Kornienko: 388–95.

Platonov, Andrei Klimentovich. 2004. *Sochineniia. Tom 1: 1918–1927 Kniga 2: Stat'i.* Moscow: IMLI RAN.

———. 2009. *Chevengur. Kotlovan. Sobranie sochinenii v 8-kh tomakh: vol 2*, ed. N. Malygina. Moscow: Vremia.

———. 2010a. *Schastlivaia Moskva. Sobranie sochinenii v 8-kh tomakh: vol 4*, ed. N. V. Kornienko. Moscow: Vremia.

———. 2010b. *Smerti net! Sobranie sochinenii v 8-kh tomakh: vol 5*, ed. N. V. Kornienko. Moscow: Vremia.

———. 2011a. *Usomnivshiisia Makar. Sobranie. sochinenii v 8-kh tomakh: vol 1* , ed. N. V. Kornienko. Moscow: Vremia.

———. 2011b. *Fabrika Literatury. Sobranie sochinenii v 8-kh tomakh: vol 8*, ed. N. V. Kornienko. Moscow: Vremia

———. 2013. *Ia prozhil zhizn'. Pis'ma (1920–1950 gg.)*. Moscow: Astrel'.

Platonov, Andrei Klimentovich, and Brian Bean. 1972. *Fro and Other Stories*. Translated by Brian Bean. Moscow: Progress Publishers.

Platonov, Andrei Klimentovich, and Robert Chandler et al. 2007. *Soul and Other Stories*. Translated by Robert and Elizabeth Chandler, with Katia Grigoruk, Angela Livingstone, Olga Meerson and Eric Naiman. New York: New York Review of Books.

———. 2009. *The Foundation Pit*. Translated by Robert and Elizabeth Chandler with Olga Meerson. New York: NYRB Classics.

———. 2012. *Happy* Moscow. Translated by Robert and Elizabeth Chandler, New York: New York Review of Books.

Platonov, Andrei Klimentovich, and Anthony Olcott. 1978. *Chevengur*. Translated by Anthony Olcott. Ann Arbor, MI: Ardis.

Platt, Kevin M. F. 1997. *History in a Grotesque Key: Russian Literature and the Idea of Revolution*. Stanford, CA: Stanford University Press.

Podroga Valerii. 1991. "Evnukh dushi. Pozitsii chteniia i mir Platonova." In *Paraleli (Rossiia – Vostok Zapad)*, vypusk 2.

Poltavtseva, N. G. 1981. *Filosofskaia proza Andreia Platonova*. Rostov-na-Donu: Izd Rostovskogo un-ta.

———. 2005. "Chevengur: Ideologiia ili utopiia." In *"Strana Filosofov" Andreia Platonova: Problemy Tvorchestva*. Moskva: IMLI-RAN, pp. 161–71.

Ross Bullock, Philip. 2004. "The Musical Imagination of Andrei Platonov." *Slavonica*, 10 (1): 41–60.

———. 2005. *The Feminine in the Prose of Andrey Platonov*. Oxford: Legenda.

Sá Cavalcante Schuback, Marcia. 2017. "Kommunismens sömn – noter om Platonovs Dzjan." In *Andrej Platonov: Revolution och Existens*, ed. Tora Lane. Stockholm: Ersatz.

Sandomirskaja, Irina. 2017. "Den fördömda lyckan, eller Socialismens ekonomiska problem i Moskva." In *Andrej Platonov: Revolution oh Existens*, ed. Tora Lane. Stockholm: Ersatz.

Schmitt, Carl. 1996. *The Concept of the Political*. Translated by George Schwab. Chicago: University of Chicago Press.

Seifrid, Thomas. 1992. *Andrei Platonov. Uncertainties of Spirit*. Cambridge, UK: Cambridge University Press.

———. 1996. "Platonov, Socialist Realism, and the Avant-Garde." In *Laboratory of Dreams. The Russian Avant-Garde and Cultural Experiment*, ed. John E. Bowlt and Olga Matich, 235–44. Stanford, CA: Stanford University Press.

Shubin, Lev. 1987. *Poiski smysla otdel'nogo i obshchego sushchestvovaniia*. Moscow: Sovetskii Pisatel'.

Skakov, Nariman. 2014. "Soul Incorporated." *Slavic Review*, 73 (4): 772–800.

Teskey, Ayleen. 1982. *Platonov and Fedorov: The Influence of Christian Philosophy on a Soviet Writer*. Amersham, UK: Avebury.

———. 1985. "Platonov Criticism Since 1958. A Comparison of Soviet and Émigré Attitudes."

Turbin, V. 1965. "Misteriia Andreia Platonova." *Molodaia gvardiia*. 7: 293–307.

Varava, V. V. (ed.). 2014. *Andrei Platonov. Filosofskoe delo. Sbornik nauchnykh statei*. Voronezh: Izd. dom voronezhskogo gosudarstvennogo universiteta.

Viugin, V. Iu. 2004. *Andrei Platonov: Poetika zagadki. Ocherk stanovleniia i evoliutsiia stilia.* St. Peterburg: Izd. Russkogo khristianskogo gumanitarnogo instituta.

Zhunturova-Fisherman, O. 2000. Kul'turnye traditsii v povesti "Dzhan." In *"Strana filosofov" A Platonova: Problemy tvorchestva. Vypusk 4.* St Petersburg: 677–87.

Index

About the Author

Tora Lane has a PhD in Russian literature, is associate professor in comparative literature and acting research leader at CBEES, Södertörn University. She specializes in Russian modernism and Soviet literature. She has published several articles on the poetry of Tsvetaeva, the prose of Andrei Platonov, and on aesthetic issues related to Soviet literature. Her publications include *Rendering the Sublime: A Reading of the Fairy Tale Poem "The Swain" by Marina Cvetaeva* (2009) (dissertation) and *Dis-orientations: Philosophy, Literature, and the Lost Grounds of Modernity* (eds. with Marcia Sá Cavalcante Schuback).

Made in the USA
Middletown, DE
13 July 2020